Parish Church Architecture

An introduction to PARISH CHURCH ARCHITECTURE AD600-1965

Thelma M. Nye

B. T. BATSFORD LTD

First published 1965

Made and printed in Great Britain by
Jarrold and Sons Ltd, London and Norwich
for the publishers
B. T. BATSFORD LTD
4 Fitzhardinge Street, Portman Square, London W.1

To Neville

Contents

Acknowledgment

The author and publishers are indebted to the following for their willing and able work on the drawings:

Michael Foster for pages 12, 13, 15, 17, 19, 21 and 95;
Philip Mein for pages 23, 25, 27, 29, 31, 33, 97 and 98;
Michael Stokes for pages 38, 39, 41, 43, 45, 47, 49, 52, 53, 55, 57, 58, 60, 61, 63, 65, 67, 69, 76 and 103;
Matthew Wright for pages 35, 73, 80, 81, 82, 83, 85, 87, 89, 91 and 95.

The author would like to thank Mr Jack Stroud Foster FRIBA for reading the typescript and for his valuable help and advice.

Thanks are also due to the many architects and clergymen who have loaned photographs and plans and have supplied information.

Liturgy and Architecture

The term liturgy refers to all forms of corporate worship officially organised by the Church. In particular it is applied to the eucharistic rite instituted by Jesus at the Last Supper when He commanded His disciples 'Do this in remembrance of me'. In order to obey this command it is necessary to have a place set apart in every village and town where the Christian community can gather for corporate worship. For this purpose parish churches came into being, of which there are now over 16,000 in existence. No two are identical and each one has its contribution to make to the history of architecture and to the life of the Church.

The eucharist being the heart of the Church's liturgy, the altar is therefore the focal point both spiritually and architecturally. Ideally suited to the Catholic form of worship and ritual is the mediaeval Gothic structure with its compartmental plan, emphasising the distinct functions of priest and laity, and giving scope for liturgical processions and the acting of religious drama.

It must be remembered that in addition to worship, the mediaeval church was used for all kinds of secular purposes, including civic meetings, financial transactions and storage. It was an age of Faith, and the people were at home in the house of God.

With the Reformation liturgical changes took place. At first the Catholic liturgy was still closely adhered to, the newly Established church remaining Catholic but Reformed. The emphasis was gradually transferred from the Sacraments to the preaching of the Word, and church buildings which had hitherto been untouched by the influence of the Renaissance found that the classical style could be adapted to suit their liturgical needs. This change in architectural style was the expression of a cultural change.

In direct contrast to the Gothic structure, with its sense of the mystical and eternal, is the house-like building of the Renaissance church, with its emphasis on the earthly and material; both structures reflecting admirably the form of worship and Faith of their times.

The initiation of the first church buildings in Saxon England is obscure. It is believed that they owe their origin to the converted local thane who would have had such a building constructed primarily for himself and his family, having his own 'chaplain' to conduct the worship.

The Councils of London and Westminster held during the twelfth century resulted in the inauguration of a system of tithes whereby a tenth part of all the produce of the parish lands, whether in money or in kind, was given to the church, a quarter of which was to be devoted to the maintenance of its fabric. Some years later it became accepted that this money should cover the maintenance of the sanctuary and chancel only, the remainder of the church building becoming the responsibility of the parishioners.

Throughout the Middle Ages a large number of churches were founded, rebuilt, or enlarged at the expense of individual patrons or guilds, or as the result of bequests left by wealthy parishioners.

With rare exceptions pre-Reformation churches are the work of many generations and the blending of successive architectural styles. With the Restoration came the advent of the individual architect who, from the age of Wren to the present day, is commissioned to design a church as a unified building within given limits of site and price.

The use of Gothic never died and in an imitative form was revived to a large extent during the nineteenth century under the influence of the Tractarians and Ecclesiologists. All attempts, however, failed to recapture a style which depended on the character and sentiments of the Middle Ages, and on the skilfully executed detail which the individual architect, without a team of craftsmen, was powerless to give.

Despite the irreparable harm the mediaeval churches have suffered at the hands of the Reformer, Puritan and Restorer, they survive as living expressions of man's endeavour to give of his best to God, and they form an unbroken record of all the finest architectural achievements of our English heritage.

Today, with the new building materials that are available, and the scientific methods of construction, a wider field of design is open to the growing number of church architects. The liturgy, however, is unchanged, and whether interpreted by Anglo-Catholic or Evangelical, the church building is a place of worship where the Sacraments are administered and where the Word of God is preached.

In order to study the architectural development of the parish church it is necessary to have some guiding principle. This development, therefore, has been classified under distinctive 'styles'. The division of the Gothic period into Early English, Decorated and Perpendicular, devised by Thomas Rickman in the nineteenth century, has become an accepted classification. It must be borne in mind, however, that there are no real limits or demarcation of styles, and that every so-called 'style' is a transition from that which preceded it and a transition to that which is its successor.

Mediaeval Architecture

Anglo Saxon 600–1066

The Anglo Saxons, as shipbuilders, were skilled in the craft of timber construction, but owing to the perishable nature of this building material little evidence of their work in timber survives today. When St Augustine came to Kent in AD 598, however, he brought with him builders and craftsmen in stone and brickwork.

The church architecture of the Anglo Saxon period was based either on the Roman basilican plan, mainly found in the south of England, or the Celtic plan which grew up in the north and west. The origin of placing the altar at the east end of the church is unknown, but since the Apostolic Constitutions of the fourth century commending this position, it has become an established, though not an enforced, tradition.

The **basilican plan** consisted of two cells: a rectangular nave, and a chancel ending in an apse where the altar, usually of stone, was placed. The nave was separated from the chancel by a lofty triple arcade. The apse was either semi-circular, as at the tenth-century church of St Nicholas Worth in Sussex(*3* and *4*), or polygonal as at St Mary's Deerhurst, Gloucestershire, and All Saints Wing, Buckinghamshire(*5*). The latter is the most complete surviving basilican church of the tenth century. The earliest churches were built between AD 600 and 675, though only portions, and in some cases only foundations, survive. These are in the Kent churches of St Mary *c.* 620 and St Pancras *c.* 600 at Canterbury, St Andrew Rochester *c.* 604, St Mary Lyminge *c.* 633, St Mary Reculver *c.* 669, and at St Peter Bradwell in Essex *c.* 654. St Mary's Reculver was demolished in 1805, but the stone columns of the triple chancel arches are preserved in the crypt of Canterbury Cathedral.

The addition of side aisles was rare in Anglo Saxon times and Brixworth, Northamptonshire, was the finest and probably the earliest example(*9*). Here, as at St Wynston's Repton, Derbyshire, they no longer survive. Aisles, however, are to be seen at Wing, Buckinghamshire, Lydd, Kent, and Great Paxton in Huntingdonshire.

The **Celtic plan**; emanating from Ireland through St Aidan, developed in the north and west of England. Smallness, simplicity, and excessive height in relation to ground area, and a lack of refinement, are characteristics of these Celtic Anglo Saxon churches. Examples survive at Escomb *c.* 640(*1* and *2*), Monkwearmouth *c.* 674, and Jarrow *c.* 684

1 Escomb, Co. Durham, c. 640

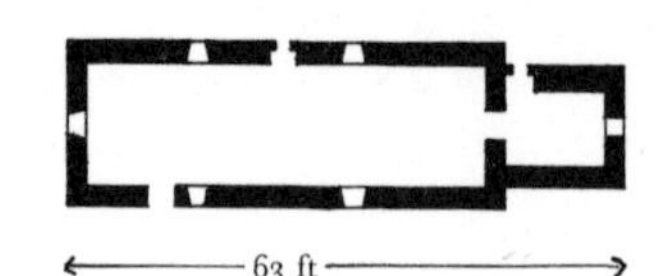

2 Plan of Escomb

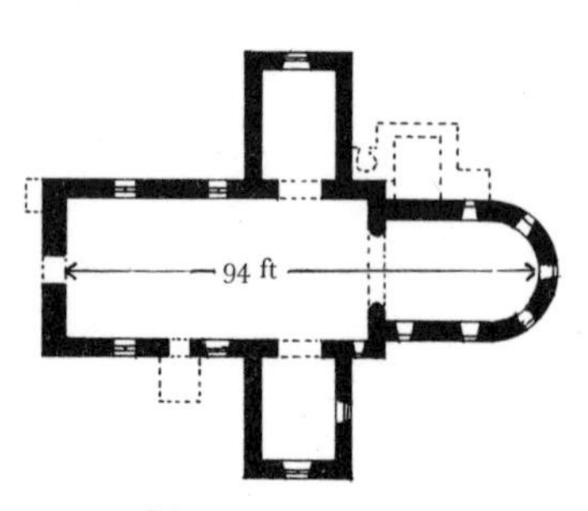

3 Plan of Worth

4 Worth, Sussex, tenth century

5 Polygonal apse, Wing, Sussex tenth century

6 Greensted, Essex, c. 845

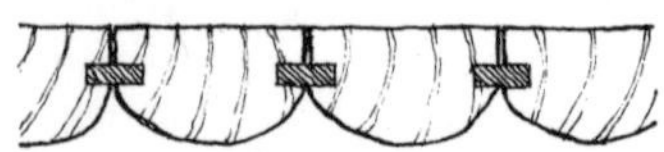

7 Transverse section of timber nave wall construction, Greensted

8 Brixworth, Northamptonshire, c. *680*

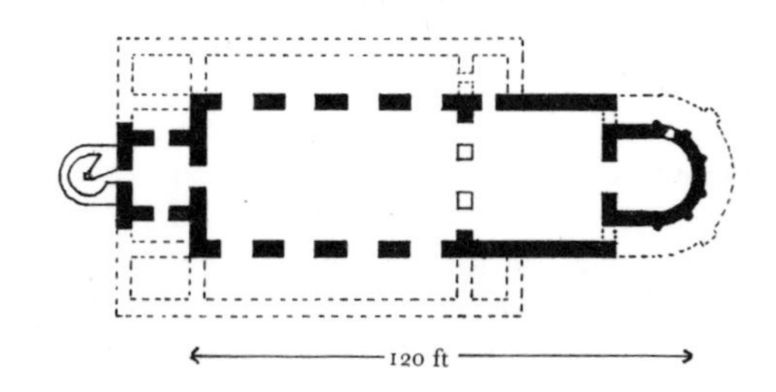

9 Plan of Brixworth

10 Eagle carved inside the south doorway at Brixworth, c. *800*

in County Durham, and in the eighth-century church of St Lawrence at Bradford on Avon, Wiltshire (*11* and *12*). This plan in its simplest form was a rectangle, with no structural division between nave and sanctuary, such as at St Peter's Heysham, Lancashire. The greatest number of churches were two-celled, constructed as two unequal oblongs, the larger forming the nave for the laity, and the smaller and narrower, the sanctuary for exclusive use by the clergy.

The nave and sanctuary were separated by a narrow archway over which, in many churches, there was a crude carving of the crucified Christ, with the figures of Mary His Mother on His right, and John the disciple on His left. The group composed what is called the *Rood*.

Timber was still used to a certain extent, and at St Andrew's Greensted, Essex, the nave wall survives as a unique example of timber building (*6*). This was constructed *c.* 845 from oak logs, split to give two outer bevels, set upright and joined together with timber pegs to form the walls (*7*).

Use was often made of Roman bricks, skilfully shaped and rich in colour, which were found in the ruins of Roman buildings, particularly in Kent and Essex. The most striking and considerable use can be seen at All Saints Brixworth, Northamptonshire *c.* 690, where Roman bricks form the great arches of the nave arcade and the smaller arches of the windows and doorways (*8*). Another example of their use is the triangular-headed west doorway of Holy Trinity Church Colchester, Essex, formed entirely of Roman bricks (*23*). The original Roman chancel arch survives at Over Denton, Cumberland. Roman bricks form the window arches of St Michael's Church, St Albans, Hertfordshire, where also the Saxon nave and chancel walls are preserved.

The **walls** of Anglo Saxon churches, although of rough rubble, were strongly, if crudely, constructed, varing in thickness from 2 to 3½ ft. They were covered with plaster made of a mixture of hair and straw, sand and lime. This was often compounded with coarsely ground tiles giving it a reddish tinge, still to be seen in parts of the masonry of the fourth-century church of St Martin, Canterbury. Only the cut stone round the windows and doorways was left unplastered, and this was generally lime-washed. Through the years most of the plaster has worn away, but some still remains at Escomb and at St Peter's Britford near Salisbury. The tower of St Mary the Virgin Sompting, Sussex (*21*) is an excellent example, showing how the thin external plaster was applied.

Traces of *herringboning*, a method of laying stone in courses inclining alternately to the left and right (*183*), can be seen in the walls at Brixworth, St Peter's Southrop, Gloucestershire, St Peter's Westhampnett, Sussex, and St Mary's York. To form the outer angles of the building, quoin stones were either laid in the characteristic long and short manner, or large square blocks of stone were piled irregularly one above the other. One of the most perfect surviving examples of the latter

11 Bradford on Avon, Wiltshire eighth century

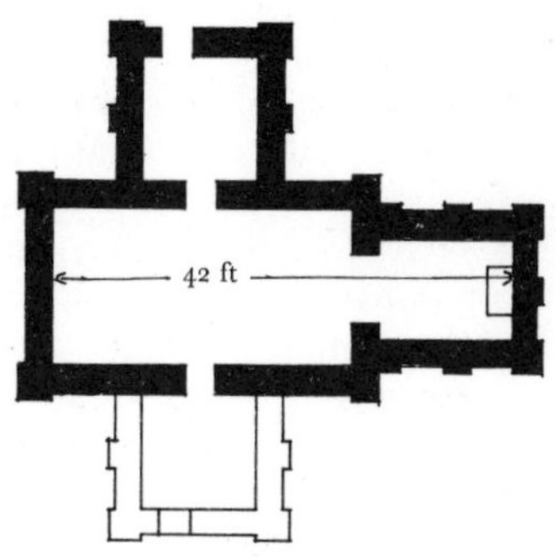

12 Plan of Bradford on Avon

13 West window of tower Caversfield Buckinghamshire

14 South window of tower Swanscombe, Kent

15 East window of tower Deerhurst, Gloucestershire

16 One of two angels carved above the chancel arch, Bradford on Avon

17 Nave window Avebury, Wiltshire

is the nave of St Peter's Bradwell, which was built almost entirely of Roman materials. Other examples are at St Mildred's Canterbury, Escomb, and Stow in Lincolnshire.

In *long and short work* a squared stone of up to 4 ft was placed vertically alternating with a flat slab set horizontally to form the corners(*182*). A clear example is seen on the tower of All Saints Earls Barton, Northamptonshire(*18*). Many other examples exist, among them the angles of Corhampton Church, Hampshire; Dunham Magna, Norfolk; North Burcombe, Wiltshire; and Brigstock, Northamptonshire.

Pilaster strips became a feature of Anglo Saxon building and consisted of flat upright stone battens varying in width from 5 to 13 ins but projecting only an inch or two from the wall. The towers of Earls Barton and Barnack, Northamptonshire, St Bene'ts Cambridge, Barton on Humber, Lincolnshire, and likewise the walls and door jambs at Corhampton and Stanton Lacey, Shropshire, show good examples. These pilaster strips are sometimes connected by arches as on the second stage of the Earls Barton tower, and on the outside wall of St Lawrence's, Bradford on Avon(*11*).

The high pitched wooden **roofs** of the Celtic churches consisted of timbers fastened together with wooden pins. In earlier churches with timber walls the roof timbers were supported on large square posts standing on sturdy pieces of wood, called *sleepers*, which rested on the floor at the foot of the wall. The timber structure was covered with slate or stone slabs laid horizontally, meeting at the top in the form of a low pyramid. Later, when the timber walls were replaced by stone, their strength made it possible to dispense with these great posts, giving more room in the church.

Towers were introduced in the tenth century. They were severe square structures usually built at the west end of the church rising and narrowing by a series of stages, each stage accentuated by a slightly projecting band of stone, called a *string course*(*18*). Often rising to over 70 ft, they served as a welcome landmark to travellers. Their primary purpose was to house the bells, but they consisted of two or more storeys which were divided by wooden floors reached by ladders. In many cases one storey would appear to have been used to house the sacristan or priest, having an opening in the east wall to enable him to see into the church. Doors and windows of these tower rooms are to be seen at Bosham, Sussex, Deerhurst, Barton on Humber, and St Bene'ts Cambridge. The belfries generally had an opening on each side of the tower. Earls Barton tower is a particularly fine example of Anglo Saxon workmanship. The belfry openings, each side divided into five spaces by turned baluster shafts, are exceptionally large and decorative(*18*). Sompting retains its unique helm spire(*21*), a construction common in the German Rhineland.

In East Anglia the towers are generally round, built of flint and rubble,

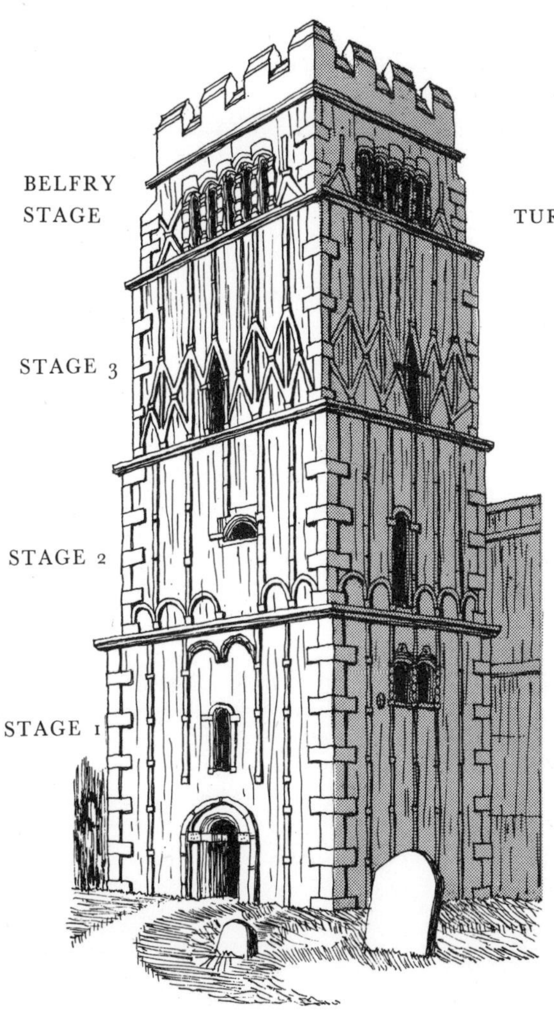

18 Earls Barton, Northamptonshire tenth-century tower

19 Detail of tower window

bonded together with mortar. Examples are at Forncett St Peter(*22*), Roughton, and Herringfleet, Norfolk.

Doorways were made as small as possible. The majority had semicircular arches and were plainly framed with square unmoulded jambs. At Monkwearmouth the jambs of the tower doorway consist of squat turned stone baluster shafts, to the bases of which are added simple carvings(*20*). High above can be seen in relief the remains of a large figure of Christ. The tower doorway of All Saints Ledsham, in the West Riding of Yorkshire, is of considerable interest. The unmoulded jambs are surrounded by a broad pilaster strip decorated with scroll work.

The doorway leading from the nave to the tower at St Bene'ts Cambridge *c.* 950, is a crude attempt by the Anglo Saxons to imitate Roman work. At St Andrew's Brigstock, Northamptonshire, there is the unusual feature of a triangular headed doorway between the tower and the turret. The main doorway was usually placed to the west end of the nave and, where there was a western tower, the ground floor was used as a porch.

Doors were of plain oak boards of double thickness placed vertically outside and horizontally inside, fastened together by long wrought iron nails with ornamental heads.

Often projecting from the main rectangular plan was a square vestibule or side chapel, called a *porticus*, an example of which survives at Bradford on Avon, where it is now used as a porch.

The points from which an arch springs, called *imposts*, were generally square projections as at Barnack(*26*), and sometimes bevelled or crudely carved as on the tower arch at Sompting(*24*) and St Bene'ts Cambridge (*25*).

Windows were small and placed high in the walls. As the walls were thick the openings were deep and, so as to give more light, the stonework was often *splayed*, i.e. shaped to slope back on either side, often both internally and externally, the window being centrally placed in the breadth of the wall. Good examples of double splayed windows are at St Nicholas's Boarhunt, Hampshire, St Peter's Diddlebury, Shropshire, St Bartholomew's Green's Norton, Northamptonshire, and St Peter and St Paul's Swanscombe, Kent(*14*). The arch of the latter is composed of Roman bricks. Single light windows splayed externally can be seen in the west walls of the towers of Wyckham, Berkshire, Woodstone, Huntingdonshire, and Caversfield, Buckinghamshire(*13*), and internally in the nave of St James's Avebury, Wiltshire(*17*).

The sides, or *jambs*, of window openings are square and unmoulded. The head was generally rounded, or triangular as in the towers at Deerhurst(*15*), Bassingham, and Herringfleet, Norfolk. The tower of St Peter's Barton on Humber has both rounded and triangular-headed openings. Glass was expensive so most window openings were unglazed and covered with parchment or oiled linen to exclude the

20 *West doorway*
Monkwearmouth, Co. Durham, c. *675*

22 *Round tower*
Forncett St Peter, Norfolk

21 *Tower, Sompting, Sussex*
eleventh century

23 *West doorway, Holy Trinity*
Colchester, Essex

wind and rain. Distinctive of the Anglo Saxon period are the two-light window openings in towers divided by a turned baluster shaft; the thickness of the wall being carried by single square stone pillars, while the baluster shaft support is set forward to the front edge of the opening. Earls Barton again provides an excellent example (*19*). Other examples are at Worth, St Mary's York, St Michael's Oxford, and Monkwearmouth. The west window at Barnack is one of the simplest Saxon windows, made up of seven stones crudely put together. In the saddleback tower of the pre-conquest church of St Martin on the Wall Wareham, Dorset, a Saxon window still survives, together with traces of long and short work. A *saddleback* is a tower roof shaped like an ordinary gabled timber roof. Occasionally a circular opening was made as in the tower of Forncett St Peter, Norfolk (*22*). These openings are double splayed and rarely exceed 9 ins in diameter.

Piers were short and stumpy with square blocks of stone at their heads and bases.

About AD 850 Pope Leo IV directed that a **piscina** should be provided near the altar for the disposal of water used for the ablutions of the chalice and patten and for the priest's hands after Mass. The earliest form of piscina is a drain hole in the floor on the south side of the chancel; and surviving examples are at Little Casterton and North Luffenham in Rutland, and Barton Bendish and Tilney All Saints in Norfolk. The Latin word *piscina* literally means 'fish pond'.

An early form of *axe* was the principal tool of the Anglo Saxons, so mouldings, carvings, and ornament were crude. In Fletton Church, Huntingdonshire, and Breedon, Leicestershire, fragments of stonework with animal ornament and figures have survived; also two angels, beautifully carved, above the chancel arch at Bradford on Avon, probably part of the original Rood (*16*); an eagle *c.* 800 inside the south doorway at Brixworth (*10*), and an eleventh-century 'Seated Christ' at Barnack. Set in the porch wall at Langford, Oxfordshire, there is a crucifix of Anglo Saxon work which was probably once part of the Rood; a figure of the Virgin and Child at Shelford, Nottinghamshire, and at Wirksworth, Derbyshire, is a remarkable carving *c.* 800 depicting scenes in the Life of Jesus.

A few Anglo Saxon churches had **crypts**; the earliest known which still survives, is that at Hexham, Northumberland, AD 675. At Brixworth only traces remain. A remarkable crypt survives at Wing, and a late seventh-century one at Repton which consists of a stone vaulted roof supported by four slender cylindrical columns with a spiral moulding round each (*27*).

Fonts were simple tubs of stone without mouldings but with an occasional crude carving. Saxon fonts survive in the churches of All Saints Little Billing, Northamptonshire (*28*) and Potterne, Wiltshire. At Deerhurst the Saxon font is said to be the best preserved in existence.

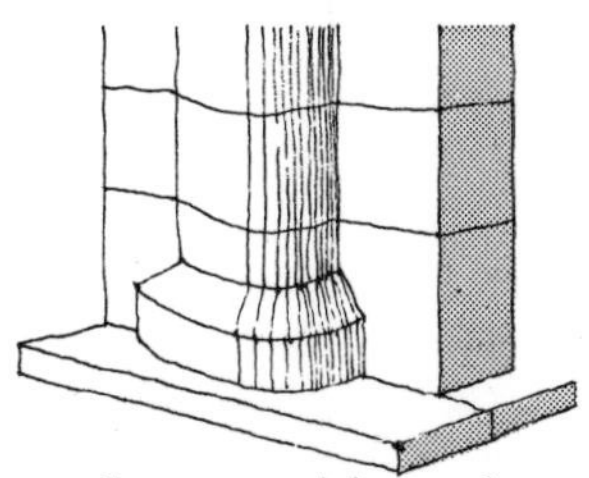

24 Impost and base of tower arch Sompting, Sussex

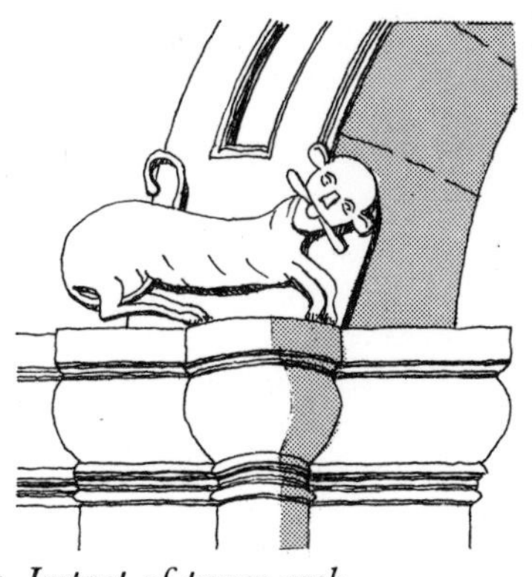

25 Impost of tower arch St Bene't's, Cambridge, tenth century

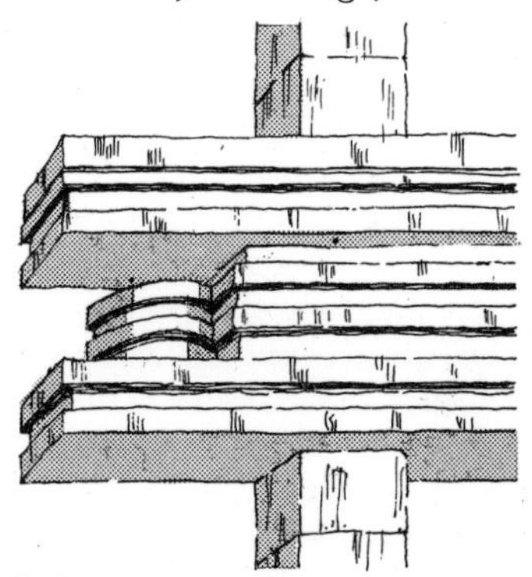

26 Impost, Barnack, Northamptonshire

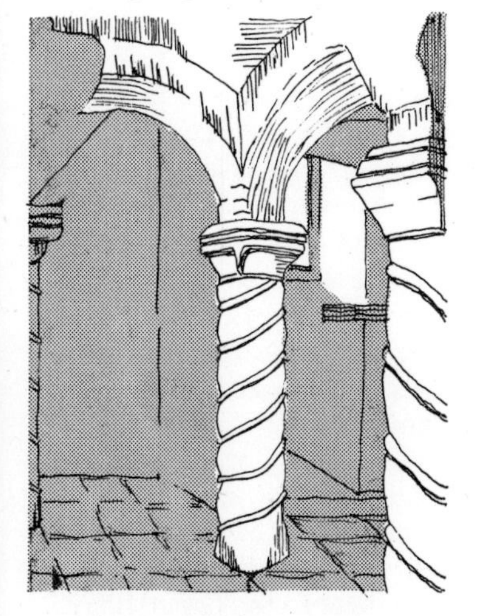

27 Crypt at Repton, Derbyshire seventh century

28 Font, Little Billing Northamptonshire

Norman 1066–1160

Following the Norman Conquest of England (1066), there slowly developed the solid and massive architecture characteristic of this period. Based on the tradition and influence of the Romans this phase of architecture throughout Europe is styled *Romanesque* and in England is referred to in particular as *Norman*. Owing to their initial preoccupation with large buildings, the Normans paid little attention to parish churches until the turn of the century. During the following fifty years the great majority of Anglo Saxon timber churches were destroyed, the stone ones reconstructed, and as a result of the spread of Christianity and the growth of population, as many as 6,000 new churches were built. Of these St Nicholas's Barfreston, Kent, St Michael and All Angels Stewkley, Buckinghamshire, and St John the Baptist Adel in the West Riding of Yorkshire, survive with very little alteration. In the majority of the other churches only portions of Norman work can be traced.

A simple two- or three-celled **plan** continued to be used for the parish church with a square or apsidal sanctuary. The two-celled church of St John the Baptist Adel, and the three-celled church of St John the Evangelist Elkstone, Gloucestershire, are examples of square-ended sanctuaries. Hales, Norfolk, is an example of a three-celled church with an apse(*36*). The apse gradually became a less frequent construction owing to the lack of technical skill of the village craftsmen.

St David's Kilpeck, Herefordshire *c.* 1160(*30* and *31*) is a typical example of a three-celled church with an apsidal sanctuary with stone vaulting, and displays both exterior and interior features which are wholly late Norman in character. It is one of the smallest churches in England and also one of the richest in sculptured ornament. On the outside walls can be seen the broad flat buttresses typical of Norman work, and beneath the eaves a projecting block of stone, called a *corbel table*, gives extra support to the roof and is carved with grotesque heads. The south doorway is worthy of particular attention(*29*). Each order of the archway is profusely carved with different ornament using beak head, grotesque heads of animals, birds and fishes. The jambs are carved with foliage, serpents and warlike figures.

Sometimes, where the sanctuary was square-ended, a central or *axial* tower was raised above the choir, as at Stewkley(*38* and *39*), and where there was an apse a west tower was constructed, as at St Mary's Birkin, Yorkshire. A rare example of both apse and western tower occurs at St Michael's Newhaven, Sussex. St Mary the Virgin Iffley, Oxfordshire *c.* 1160 is an example of an unaisled church with an axial tower and square-ended sanctuary. It is one of the most ambitious

29 South doorway
Kilpeck, Herefordshire, c. 1160

30 Kilpeck, Herefordshire, c. 1160

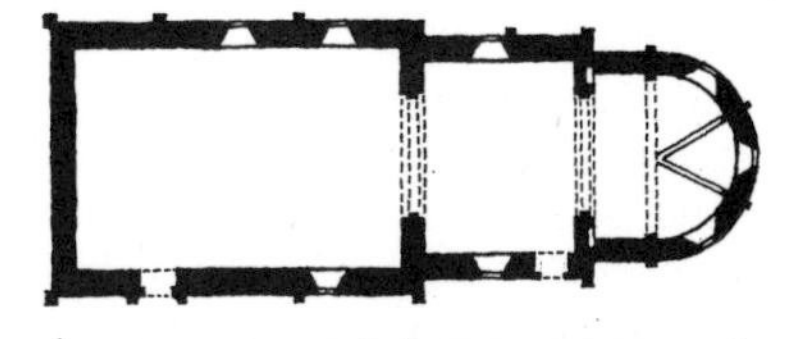

31 Plan of Kilpeck

32 Niche, Leigh, Worcestershire, c. 1120

33 Detail of chancel arch
Walsoken, Norfolk, late twelfth century

34 Detail of arch over south doorway
Iffley, Oxfordshire, c. 1160

35 Detail of beak heads, Iffley

examples of small church architecture. The doorways and window openings show abundant carving with beak head and Scandinavian designs(*35*). Where village churches were small the Normans, like the Anglo Saxons, often built a bell-cote which was constructed on the east or west gable of the nave. Good examples of this are on the little church of St Peter Stoke Orchard, Gloucestershire, Northborough and Peakirk in Northamptonshire, and Adel.

A nave without aisles was common during the twelfth century as village populations were still small and money was limited. When it became necessary to widen the church side aisles were added, usually about half the width of the nave. In order to do this sections of the walls were cut away, leaving pieces of supporting wall, called *piers*. To give more light when the aisles were added, the nave walls were heightened above the arcades, and windows built in. This is called a *clerestory*. Clerestories were comparatively rare in Norman times but good examples are at St Oswald's Filey, Yorkshire, St Andrew's Compton Bishop, Somerset, All Saints Walsoken, Norfolk, and St Margaret at Cliffe, Kent(*37*). The intermediate stage between the arches of the nave or chancel and the clerestory is called the *triforium*. The church of St Michael and St Mary Melbourne, Derbyshire, has the added feature of a passageway built in the thickness of the triforium wall; this form of construction, however, was at this time more usually confined to cathedrals.

Later in the period, to give more space to a growing congregation, the simple plan gave way to a cross-shaped or *cruciform* building with an aisleless nave. Square projecting areas, called *transepts*, were constructed between the nave and chancel which formed the cross. Often a tower was raised over the arches at the four points of intersection. This plan was not widely adopted in the smaller parish church but good examples are seen at St Nicholas's Old Shoreham, Sussex, which was converted from the simple plan, St Knyeburgha's Castor, Northamptonshire, St Nicholas's North Newbald, Yorkshire, and St John Devizes, Wiltshire. The most imposing are those churches of cruciform plan with aisles such as Melbourne and St Mary's Hemel Hempstead, Hertfordshire. The latter is the best preserved example surviving today. The earliest part is the relatively low chancel *c.* 1150, which is rib-vaulted.

There were, of course, exceptions to these plans and a few churches, such as those dedicated to The Holy Sepulchre at Cambridge and Northampton, are circular, being based on the church of The Holy Sepulchre in Jerusalem from which returning Crusader knights derived their inspiration.

Central **towers** are square, low and sturdy, and unlike the Anglo Saxon ones were not constructed to carry bells. They had a single row of windows and were called *lantern towers*. Towards the end of the period these central towers were made higher by the addition of a belfry on the

36 Hales, Norfolk, twelfth century

37 St Margaret at Cliffe, Kent

38 Stewkley, Buckinghamshire, twelfth century

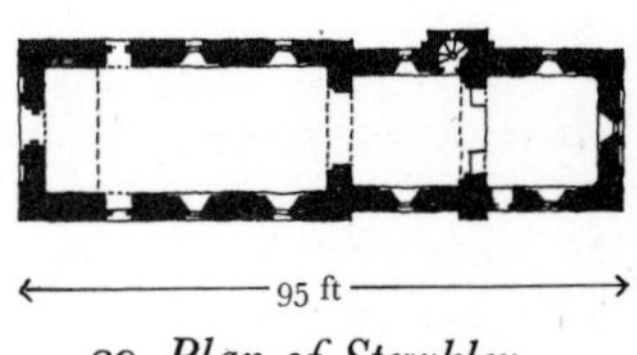

39 Plan of Stewkley

top. Where there was no central tower, a tower was often formed by raising the walls of the existing western porch, as at Brixworth and St Pancras's Canterbury (of which now only the ruins of the church remain). In East Anglia round towers still prevailed, with walls generally 4 to 5 ft thick, of flint bound together with rough durable mortar. Towers often had the addition of a small turret containing a stone spiral staircase.

All the original tower roofs have now disappeared. These were generally a low pyramidal capping of timber, protected by a covering of wood shingle. An example of a saddleback construction survives at St Michael's Duntisbourne Rous, Gloucestershire, and an unusual feature of a double saddleback is at St Bartholomew's Fingest, Buckinghamshire.

Walls were generally thicker than those of the Anglo Saxon period, and were usually constructed of small stones with a core of rubble (*184*). Herringbone masonry (*183*) was used to a greater extent than in Anglo Saxon times, and a good example is seen on the tower at Carlton in Lindrick, Nottinghamshire. As the masons grew in skill the stone wall arcade became a favourite feature of structural, as well as of ornamental, importance. In parish churches it appears mainly on the towers and west fronts. Towards the end of the Norman period these arcades were richly carved and a fine example is the interlacing arches on the west front of St Lawrence's Castle Rising, Norfolk (*40*). Other examples are at Melbourne, Walsoken and Tilney All Saints, and the tower at Castor *c.* 1124 (*52*). The chancel at Stow is another example.

Broad flat **buttresses** take the place of pilaster strips as at Hampton in Arden, Warwickshire, Newhaven, Kilpeck, Iffley (*51*) and Monk's Horton, Kent (*53*), but they remain purely ornamental, generally of a single stage finishing in a slope under the cornice.

String courses were often carried round the building below the sills of windows internally as well as externally. They were chamfered as at Iffley, ornamented as at Stewkley, or moulded as at Dorchester.

For **roof** construction timber was the cheapest and technically the easiest material to handle. Norman roofs were normally of steep pitch with tie beams placed very close together. On the underside was nailed a flat boarded ceiling.

The tendency for timber roofs to catch fire led to experiments with stone. The simplest and oldest form of stone roofing is the semi-circular or barrel vault, examples of which survive in the Norman chancel at St Mary's Kempley, Gloucestershire, and the nave of Copford, Essex, *c.* 1130. A *barrel vault* (*185*) is a continuous rounded arch of stone constructed over a very strong wooden frame, called *centering*, which is removed when the mortar is set. This type of construction was confined to small low areas and was therefore mainly used for crypt vaulting.

A *groined vault* (*186*), formed by the intersection of two barrel vaults

40 West front, Castle Rising, Norfolk, c. *1160*

at right-angles one to the other, can be seen in the chancel at Coln St Denis, Gloucestershire, Darenth, Kent, Studland, Dorset, and St John Devizes, Wiltshire (*41*). Groined vaulting also forms the aisle roof in the completely preserved church at Blythe, Nottinghamshire, and over the apse at Steetley, Derbyshire.

Towards the end of the Norman period more complicated structures were used, such as the *quadripartite* (four-celled) type, showing the first use of the central boss as at Elkstone and Hemel Hempstead, and the *sexpartite* (six-celled) type of which a unique example survives in the chancel at Tickencote, Rutland, the remaining part of this church having been reconstructed.

A few Norman **gable crosses** are preserved, such as at St Margaret's York, St Michael's Othery, Somerset (*49*), and St Germain's, Cornwall (*50*).

Piers consist of a shaft, capital and base. During the early part of the Norman period piers were massive, sometimes perfectly square, as at Bakewell, Derbyshire, but generally they were cylindrical with cushion or volute type **capitals** below a square, flat slab of stone, called an *abacus*, the under edge of which was bevelled or chamfered. This style was characteristic of all work prior to 1090. Later, octagonal piers were constructed, their capitals often formed with heavy scallops or crude carvings of animals and foliage or biblical scenes, as at Adel (*57*). At Selby, Yorkshire, the capitals are carved with Celtic basket work. Alternating cylindrical and octagonal columns became a feature of late Norman work and this arrangement was carried into the Transitional period.

The north nave arcade of Pittington, Co. Durham, displays spiral and moulded variations of column decoration, the capitals being carved with scallops. St Mary Stourbridge, Worcestershire (*54*), Walsoken, Norfolk, and Stanley St Leonard, Gloucestershire, also show excellent examples of scalloped capitals. Simple cushion type capitals can be seen at Ickleton, Cambridgeshire, and Cassington, Oxfordshire. A carved cushion type capital and one with angle volutes can be seen together in St Peter's Northampton (*55* and *56*).

The **bases** of the piers are square and low with a flattened roll-moulding at the foot of the shaft. They stand on a square **plinth.** Sometimes the corners are decorated with a leaf carving as in the chapel at Postlip, Northamptonshire *c.* 1150 (*58*).

All arches were invariably round and emphasised by concentric recessed rings of stone, called *orders*. In the early Norman period these were left unmoulded, but later there was a marked development in moulding which became elaborately carved with such designs as the chevron or zig-zag, the billet which was a motif made up of short raised rectangles placed at regular intervals, and beak head (*35*). Outstanding examples are the chancel arches at Stoneleigh, Warwickshire,

41 Stone vaulted chancel
St John's Devizes, Wiltshire, twelfth century

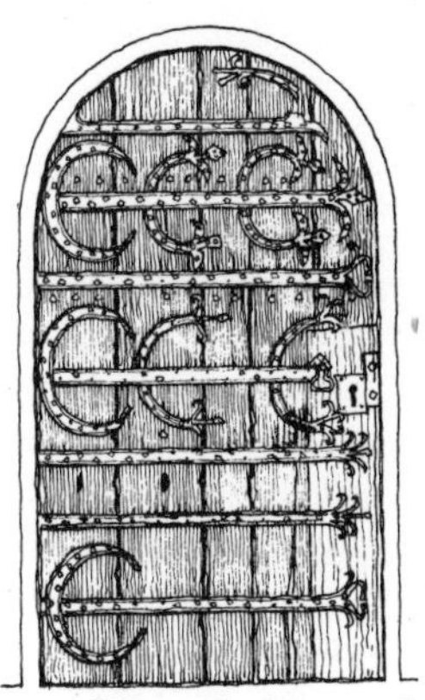

42 Wrought ironwork on south door
Hartley, Kent

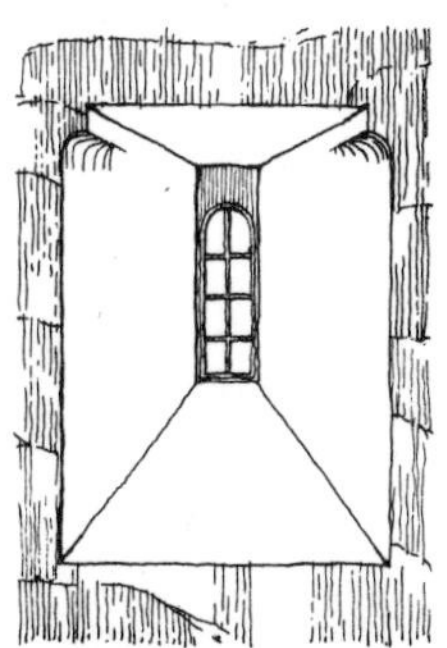

Interior view

Exterior view

43 and 44 Handborough, Oxfordshire

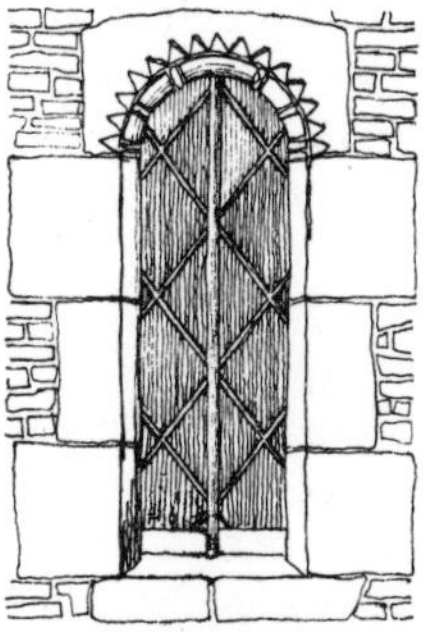

45 East window, Darenth
Kent

46 East window
Beaudesert, Warwickshire

47 Circular window
St James's, Bristol

Walsoken, Norfolk (*33*), Wakerley, Northamptonshire, and Winchfield, Hampshire.

Horseshoe shaped arches are occasionally seen as in the aisles of St Bartholomew's Smithfield, London, and Holywell, Oxfordshire *c.* 1100 (*60*).

The main entrance to the Norman parish church was a doorway generally to the south of the nave and the western tower was solely a belfry. The south side was chosen because this was invariably the side nearest to the village.

The south **doorway** was in many cases the most elaborate part of the small church, with its deep projection of walling and elaborately carved orders which often continued to the ground on either side. Steetley, Derbyshire, and Quenington, Gloucestershire, have fine examples; also St Bees, Cumberland. Some doorways had a carved panel under the arch, called a *tympanum*. The carving was generally crude and grotesque, depicting fabulous monsters and biblical scenes of doom and judgment. Examples are at Brinsop, Herefordshire, Ault Hucknall, Derbyshire, and Pipe Aston, Herefordshire (*48*).

Doors were of oak to which wrought iron hinges, locks, handles and knockers added beauty as well as strength. Fine examples survive at St Margaret's Leicester, St Edward the Confessor's Westcot Barton, Oxfordshire, All Saints Campton, Bedfordshire, St Mary's Merton, Surrey, and All Saints Hartley, Kent (*42*). The door of St Mary's Haddiscoe, Norfolk, is almost wholly covered with angular strapwork from which branch multitudinous scrolls.

Porches were generally shallow and had not become a recognised feature in Norman times. Examples, however, can be seen at Balderton, Nottinghamshire, Adel, and Brixworth.

Niches, in which sculptured figures were placed, were sometimes seen over doorways and between arches. An example is at Leigh, Worcestershire (*32*).

During the early part of the Norman period the **windows** remained small, often no more than slits, and were placed high in the walls. They were of simple construction, as at Darenth, Kent (*45*) and East Barnet, Hertfordshire.

Examples are rare, as apart from those in belfry towers most have been replaced by larger ones. The stonework was deeply splayed to give more light, and a good example of this can be seen at St Peter and St Paul's Handborough, Oxfordshire *c.* 1120 (*43* and *44*). Single window lights often had arcading decorating solid walls, called *blind arcading*, on either side as at Castle Rising and Old Shoreham. With the increased skill of the masons, double windows with a central shaft or mullion were introduced. In the larger churches the wheel window became a feature of Norman work, such as at Barfreston, Kent, which is divided by shafts into segments, and St James's Bristol (*47*). Late Norman windows

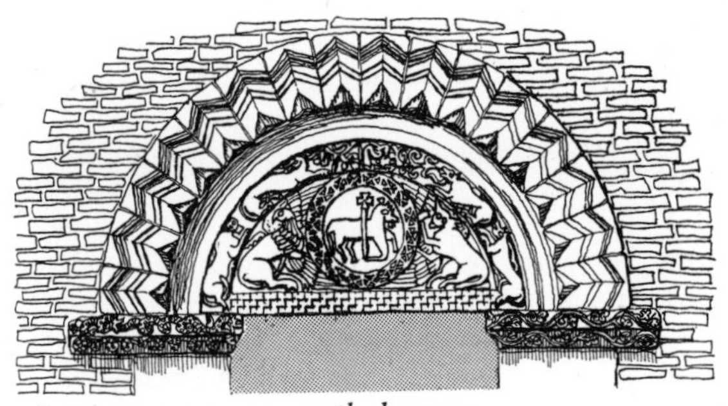

48 Tympanum over north doorway
Pipe Aston, Herefordshire

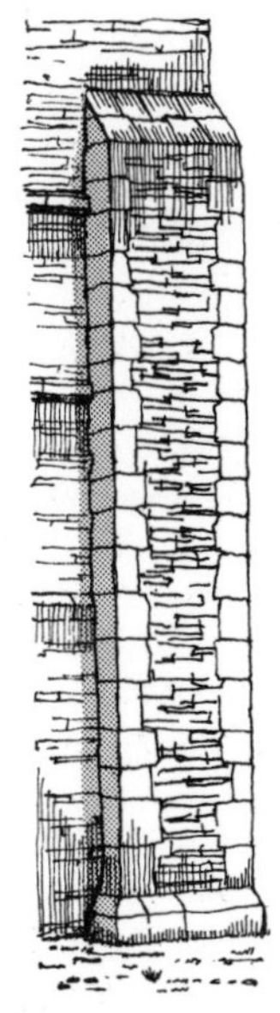

Gable crosses

49 Othery, Somerset

50 St Germain
Cornwall

51 Buttress
Iffley, Oxfordshire
c. *1160*

52 Detail of tower
Castor, Northamptonshire

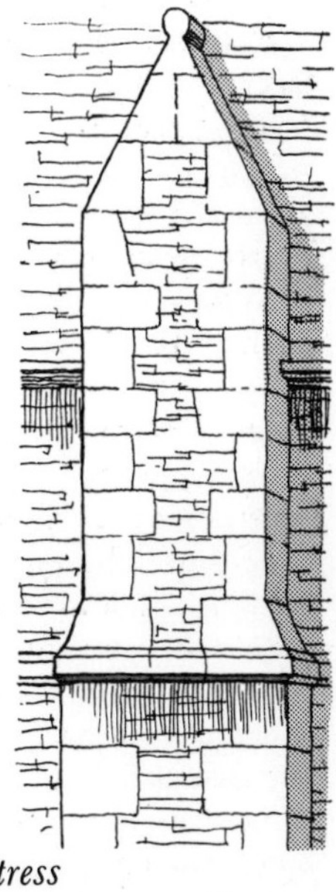

53 Buttress
Monk's Horton, Kent, c. *1180*

show magnificent carving as in that surrounding the west window at Elkstone *c.* 1180, and Beaudesert, Warwickshire (*46*).

From the twelfth century a window-like opening in the south wall of the chancel, known as a *low side window*, became a common feature. It was an unglazed opening fitted with a wooden shutter or grating. Its original function remains a matter of conjecture and it was possibly used purely for ventilation. Such an opening, still retaining its shutter, can be seen at All Saints Rampton, Cambridgeshire.

From the twelfth century onwards the **sedilia** became a permanent structure in the chancel consisting of three recessed seats in the south wall for use by the celebrant, deacon and sub-deacon during Mass. The arches over their heads were generally simply carved with chevron, as at St Mary de Castro, Leicester (*61*). It is possible that sedilia of wood existed although no signs of their construction survive.

The **piscina** was frequently incorporated in the design of the sedilia, making four rounded arches. The *pillar piscina* was fairly common, consisting of a stone shaft supporting a small basin draining directly to the ground outside, as at St Mary's Yatton, Somerset. A simple single wall piscina can be seen at Crowmarsh, Oxfordshire (*59*).

Interiors of walls were generally painted and the earliest known painting is at Patcham, Sussex *c.* 1180, depicting the Doom. A painting of the Apostles survives at Kempley, Gloucestershire, and The Ladder of Salvation at Chaldon, Surrey.

A **crypt**, normally sited below the chancel or sanctuary, was an important feature of church planning until the end of the Norman period, and consisted of narrow gangways and chambers, similar to the catacombs in Rome. Of the few surviving, that at Lastingham, Yorkshire *c.* 1080 is probably the earliest. Others are at St Mary's Warwick, and St Mary le Bow, Cheapside, London. The crypt of St John the Baptist's Berkswell, Warwickshire *c.* 1150 is divided into two bays roofed with quadripartite vaulting.

Norman **fonts** are numerous, displaying crudely carved details. Early ones are tubs of stone often decorated with shafts with cushion capitals. Fine examples of Norman fonts are at Ancaster, Lincolnshire *c.* 1140, Torpenhow, Cumberland, and Chaddesley Corbett, Worcestershire *c.* 1140 (*62*).

The font at Burnham Deepdale, Norfolk, has a series of panels depicting the twelve months of the year, and that at Raunds, Northamptonshire has a book rest carved in the form of a ram's head. Unusual fonts of black marble, imported from Tournai in Belgium, survive at East Meon, Hampshire, St Peter's Ipswich, Suffolk, and Thornton Curtis, Lincolnshire.

The earliest **tombs** to be seen in the twelfth century in parish churches are simple stone slabs, incised with a cross, usually running full length of the slab.

*54 Scalloped capital
Stourbridge
Cambridgeshire,* c. *1120*

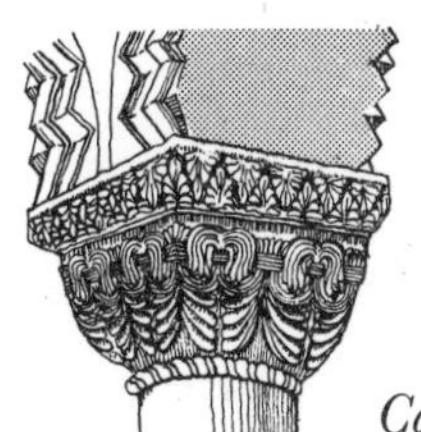

*Carved capitals
55 and 56 St Peter's, Northampton,* c. *1180*

*57 Capital of chancel arch
Adel, Yorkshire*

*58 Base, Postlip Chapel
Northamptonshire,* c. *1150*

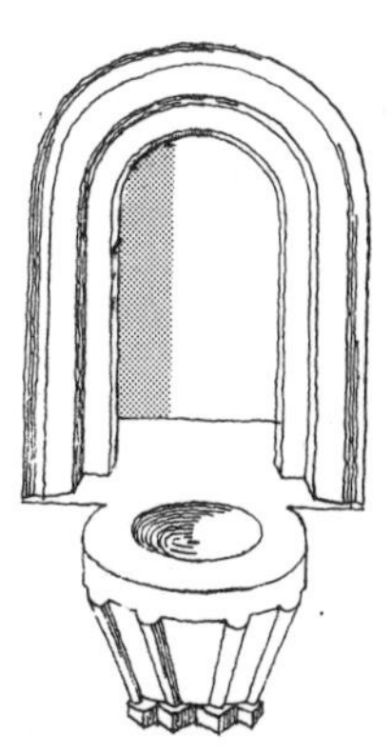

*59 Piscina, Crowmarsh
Oxfordshire*

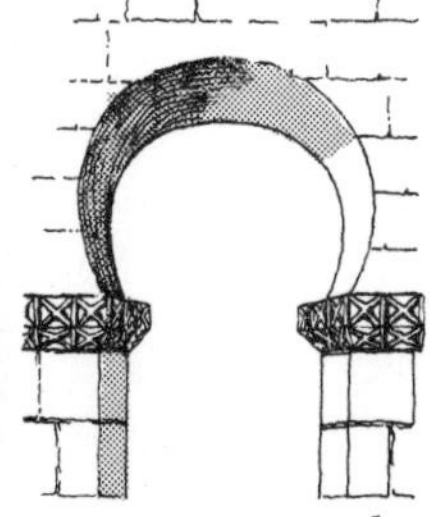

*60 Horseshoe archway
Holywell, Oxfordshire,* c. *100*

61 Sedilia, St Mary de Castro, Leicester

*62 Font, Chaddesley Corbett
Worcestershire,* c. *1140*

Transitional 1160–1200

During the last half of the twelfth century there was a movement towards elegance and refinement in church architecture: a transition between the massive Norman and the delicate Gothic, in which both styles are apparent. The Cistercian Order with its insistence on simplicity, together with the surviving Celtic tradition in the north, did much to influence church planning during this period.

The two-celled **plan** with aisled nave, and less frequently the cruciform plan, with or without a central tower, remained in common use throughout the Middle Ages.

The problem of stone vaulting was at last mastered and although this in itself was not to influence the architecture of the parish church, the style to which it led was to have a supreme effect.

From the early barrel vault(*185*) emerged the groined vault(*186*) and later the *ribbed vault*. The latter was formed by a frame in the shape of six arches, four connecting with adjoining pillars, and two crossing the frame diagonally(*187*). This was a much stronger construction and easier to make but was limited to small low areas. The introduction of the pointed arch(*188*) proved the solution to all the difficulties and the most marked feature of the Transitional period is the emergence of the pointed arch, which is seen side by side with the round headed arches of the Normans. Characteristic of this period is the mingling of new forms with old. This tendency is generally most apparent in arcades between nave and aisle, and the chancel archways. The late Norman use of alternating circular piers with octagonal piers of the Early English style is also a distinctive feature of the transition.

Good examples of Transitional work can be seen all over the country, but no one church survives where it strongly prevails. The church of St Nicholas Castle Hedingham, Essex, is a fine example. Its nave arcade *c.* 1180, rests on alternating circular and octagonal piers(*65*) with splendidly carved capitals showing the beginning of the Early English *stiff-leaf foliage*. This name is given as the stiff stalks to the leaves rise from the ring of the capital, the leaves themselves curling over in a graceful manner(*73*). A similar construction and arrangement of piers are seen in the nave arcades at Walsoken and Tilney All Saints, Norfolk, and at Worksop, Nottinghamshire. The nave arcades at Barnack are semicircular. The columns of the north arcade *c.* 1175, are circular with chevron ornament, characteristic of the Norman period, and those of the south arcade *c.* 1185 have clustered piers of eight shafts which is characteristic of the Early English style. This shows clearly the progress made in the course of ten years. Clustered piers and pointed arches are also seen at Little Dunmow, Essex *c.* 1200.

63 New Shoreham, Sussex, c. *1200*

64 West doorway
Rothwell, Northamptonshire

65 Alternating octagonal and circular piers
Castle Hedingham, Essex, c. *1180*

At Warmington, Northamptonshire, cushion capitals support pointed arches, and at Polebrooke, Northamptonshire, rounded arches have deep hollow mouldings of the Early English period. Pointed chancel arches with Norman mouldings are seen at Soham, Cambridgeshire, Blosham, Oxfordshire, and Clevedon, Somerset. At Broadwater in Sussex the eastern arch of the central tower is semi-circular and the western is pointed; both are enriched with Norman chevron ornament.

Another fine example of Transitional work is the cruciform church at New Shoreham, Sussex (*63*), which was constructed *c.* 1175–1200 and has the unusual feature of aisles full length of both nave and chancel. The belfry has round openings contained within pointed arches.

Walls were still thick but were constructed of more carefully worked stones.

Buttresses remained shallow in projection and of little structural significance.

Windows tended to be made larger, were more deeply splayed, and increased in number.

Doorways began to show the pointed arch as at St Mary's Ely *c.* 1200. The west doorway of Rothwell, Northamptonshire (*64*) has a pointed arch with its orders enriched with chevron and semi-hexagonal mouldings. The shafts of the jambs are banded and have capitals of stiff-leaf foliage.

The cylindrical **piers** gave way to more slender columns, and traces of Early English work are seen in the ball-like volutes of capitals on the nave arcades at Barnack, Duddington and Polebrooke, Northamptonshire.

Bases became more elaborate, as at St Cross, Hampshire *c.* 1160 where the corners are decorated with a leaf motif.

The use of the *chisel* made possible a greater refinement of ornament and the edges of each order in the arches were chamfered, producing a much softer effect. More delicate waterleaf and stiff-leaf foliage superseded the heavy scalloped capitals and these can be seen to perfection at Bledlow Church Buckinghamshire, and Kimpton, Hertfordshire. The waterleaf is a broad, unribbed, tapering leaf curving up towards the angle of the abacus and turned in at the top.

Dating from the Transitional period is the **crypt** below the sanctuary at Newark, Nottinghamshire. It is about 20 ft square, consisting of three bays with quadripartite vaulting.

Fonts are very similar to those of Norman times, the octagonal shape being the most common.

Early English 1200–1300

In contrast to the sturdiness of Norman architecture there evolved through the Transitional period the slender, graceful and dignified churches of Early English workmanship. This period, together with the Decorated of the fourteenth century and the Perpendicular of the fifteenth and sixteenth centuries, form what is known as the *Gothic* period of architecture.

The Early English style is distinctively marked by the pointed arch and the growing lightness of structure, lancet windows(*79*), detached shafts and capitals carved with stiff-leaf foliage(*73*), water hold mouldings on the bases(*77*), double doorways(*67*), and the free use of dog-tooth ornament(*69*).

The purity of the Early English style is best seen in the cathedrals; fine examples, however, survive in parish churches of which the large building of St Mary's West Walton, Norfolk, is one of the best. Others are at St Mary's Eaton Bray, Bedfordshire, the cruciform church of St Mary Potterne, Wiltshire, and the small rectangular planned church of St Giles Skelton in the North Riding of Yorkshire, which is a real gem of Early English work. A perfect example of the fully developed Early English style can be seen in the north transept arcade at Hexham, Northumberland.

The parish church was by now the recognised centre of the community. Not only was it a place of worship and a 'theatre' for religious drama and liturgical processions, but it was also used for all kinds of secular purposes.

The basic **plan** remained simple, either rectangular or cruciform, and many apses were lengthened into square-ended sanctuaries as at St Andrew's Tangmere, Sussex.

As the growth of population demanded, aisles were added to existing churches: lateral expansion is one feature which distinguishes the parish church development from that of the cathedral. Transepts proved impracticable, as all sight of the chancel was obscured, so they could only be usefully used as chapels. In every church by the thirteenth century the sanctuary and chancel were separated from the nave by a screen over which was carved the life-size figures of the rood (see page 14), which was supported by a substantial timber beam across the screen. Except during a service the door of the screen was kept locked, once again emphasising the separateness of the sanctuary.

In some churches it became necessary to heighten the nave walls and insert clerestory windows to give more light. These windows were often plain circles, as at Acton-Burnell, Shropshire, or trefoils or quatrefoils enclosed in a circle, as at All Saints Hargrave, Northamptonshire. A

E
S
N
W
11
5
6
3
1
9
16
10
15
14
18
1 Altar
2 Sanctuary
3 Reredos
4 Altar rails
5 Piscina
6 Sedilia
7 Window tracery
8 Mullions
9 Chancel
10 Vestry

66 Cut-away interior of a Gothic parish church

11 *Doom painting*
12 *Rood*
13 *Rood loft*
14 *Nave*
15 *Pulpit*
16 *Lectern*
17 *Parclose screen*
18 *Transept*
19 *Clerestory*
20 *Pier*
21 *Nave arcade*
22 *Font*
23 *Two-storey porch*
24 *Corner buttress*
25 *Tower*
26 *Battlemented parapet*

clerestory, however, was not a common feature until the following century.

During the thirteenth century the local guilds, many of which were very wealthy, founded their own particular chapels such as those of the mercers, dyers, cappers, and smiths at Holy Trinity, Coventry.

In the case of small buildings, when additional space became essential it was sometimes necessary to reconstruct an aisle or enlarge an existing chapel.

Walls were steadily reduced in thickness and constructed of stones cut with greater skill, although still having a core of rubble. In order to give the thinner walls adequate strength to withstand the sideways thrust of arches, or to take the load from the roof, solid **buttresses** of greater projection, but less broad, were built to take these loads. This enabled the wall area to be reduced and the window space increased.

Buttresses generally terminated in a slope under the cornice, as at Ensham, Oxfordshire *c.* 1120 (*71*), or with a triangular head or pinnacle as at Higham Ferrers, Northamptonshire.

The **string courses** project slightly, marking the different stages of the building, and have two or three mouldings.

Roofs are normally steep in pitch and it is likely that the ordinary tie beam construction (*190*) was the usual method of spanning large areas, as at St Martin's Leicester. Strong timbers, called *tie beams*, were placed at intervals from wall to wall and on their ends rested the principal rafters which were given added support at the top by a king post standing in the centre of the tie beam (*190*), or two queen posts placed near the ends. Where timbers of sufficient length were not available for tie beams, the rafters were supported at the foot by struts and tied together near the ridge by horizontal collar beams (*190*). An example of this is at Long Stanton, Cambridgeshire.

Owing to the decay of timber few of the original roof structures survive and these are mainly in Sussex. At St Nicholas's Old Shoreham a tie beam roof with dog-tooth cut on the angles survives; also one at Upmarden (*76*). Portions of roofs of this type occur and although mutilated, retain sufficient of their original character to mark their date. Tie beam and braces remain of the roof at South Moreton, Berkshire. Pamber, Hampshire, has its original circular braces above a flat plaster ceiling.

Timber roofs were commonly left open, depending for their effect chiefly on the lines of the structure and the mouldings of the heavier timber, as at Stow, Lincolnshire. In some cases a flat ceiling concealed the upper structure and at Warmington, Northamptonshire, a beautiful wooden ceiling is constructed imitating a stone vault.

Gable crosses are not very common but particularly good examples are at Little Ponton and Morton (*86*), Lincolnshire.

The earliest **aisles** were often only narrow passages and were

67 *West double doorway*
St Cross, Hampshire, c. 1250

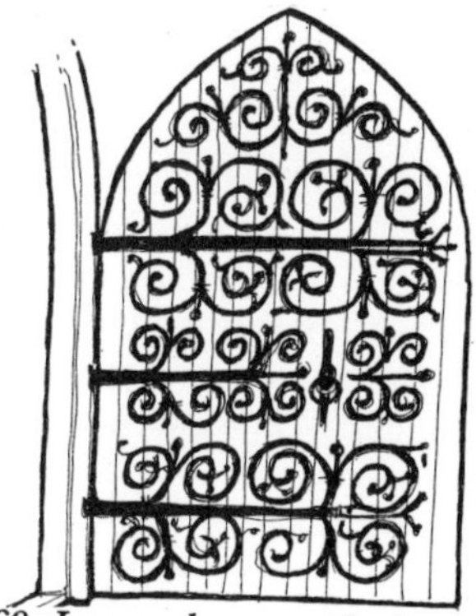

68 *Ironwork on south doorway*
Eaton Bray, Bedfordshire

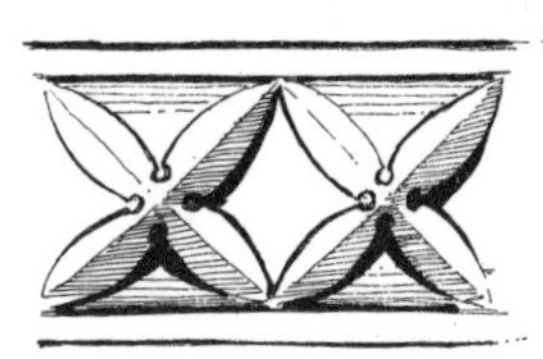

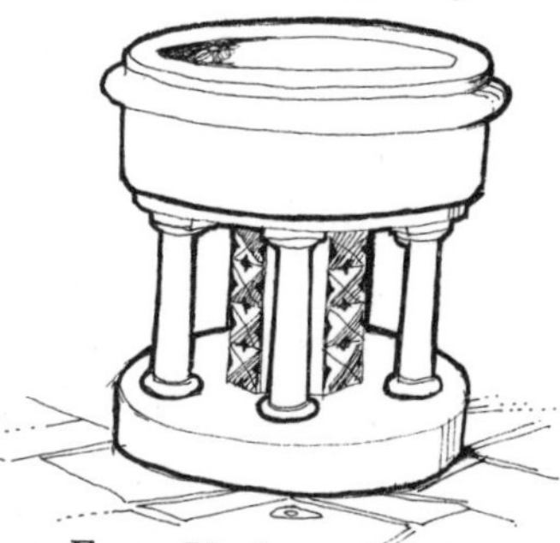

70 *Font, Hexham, Northumberland*

69 *Detail of dog-tooth ornament*

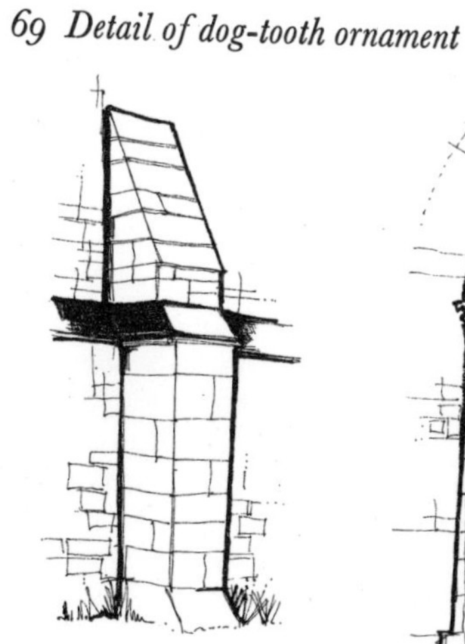

71 *Buttress, Ensham, Oxfordshire*, c. 1220

72 *West doorway*
Higham Ferrers, Northamptonshire, c. 1260

frequently contained beneath the continuous slope of the nave roof, which was of necessity low. An example is at St Michael's Amberley, Sussex.

An outstanding feature of church building in the thirteenth century was the construction of **tower** and **spire**. The spire was conceived as an integral part of the tower, and where a tower already existed a unified design was evolved. The majority of spires were octagonal and the junction at which they fitted on to a four-sided tower was disguised either by the use of a parapet, usually battlemented or by *broaches*. The latter were formed by building wedge-shaped arches across the inner corners of the tower to support the remaining four sides of the spire. These were covered by buttresses in the shape of pyramids, called *broaches*. One of the earliest broach spires is at Sleaford, Lincolnshire. Other later examples are at Ketton, Rutland, Threckingham, Lincolnshire and Raunds, Northamptonshire. The 'heaviness' of the broach spire was usually relieved by gabled windows, and often pinnacles were used at the corners of the tower; also as a means of masking the division, as at Witney, Oxfordshire and Pilton, Northamptonshire.

To drain rain water from behind a parapet, lead spouts were inserted into long projections of stone, called *gargoyles*, in the parapet walls. These were often carved with grotesque heads.

Piers are cylindrical or octagonal, frequently formed by a central pillar with detached shafts grouped round. This formation became a distinguishing feature of Early English work. An excellent example, at Eaton Bray, Bedfordshire, consists of eight shafts over which the arches are moulded with bold curves and deep hollows. They are constructed of solid blocks of skilfully cut stone, fitted tightly together. The detached shafts are usually of polished limestone or Purbeck marble, but the latter is seldom found in the parish church at this time. The shafts are tied back to the pillar by bonding stones making characteristic rings, called *annulets*, at intervals up their length.

Capitals are commonly moulded as at Irthlingborough, Northamptonshire (*74*), called *bell capitals*. Many examples exist, however, showing a variety of conventional stiff-leaf foliage such as at Stone in Kent, Eaton Bray and Ivinghoe, Buckinghamshire. Stiff-leaf foliage and carving of human heads appear on the capitals at St Mary Magdalen Sutton in Ashfield, Nottinghamshire, and the exquisite work seen at West Walton, Norfolk is considered the finest in any English parish church (*73*). The **abacus** is usually composed of roll mouldings divided by deep hollows.

Bases of the piers have a characteristic hollow between two roll mouldings and this is known as a *water hold moulding*. An early example is on the base of the south door of Stanwick, Northamptonshire *c.* 1220 (*77*). No fixed form of seating was introduced until the fourteenth

73 Capital
West Walton, Norfolk, c. 1240

74 Capital, Irthlingborough
Northamptonshire

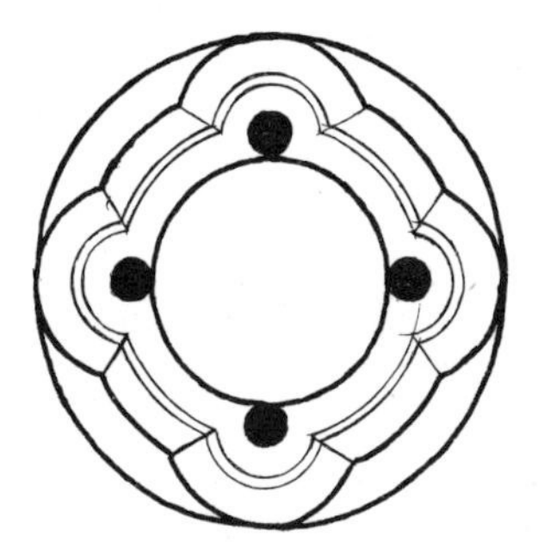

75 Section of pier, West Walton

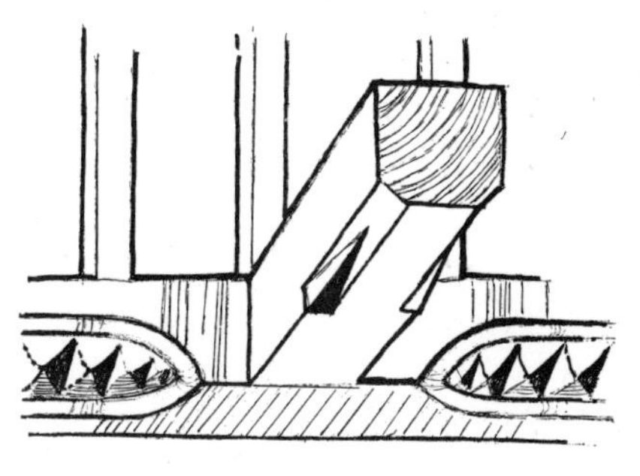

76 Detail of roof
Upmarden, Sussex, c. 1220

77 Base, south door
Stanwick, Northamptonshire, c. 1200

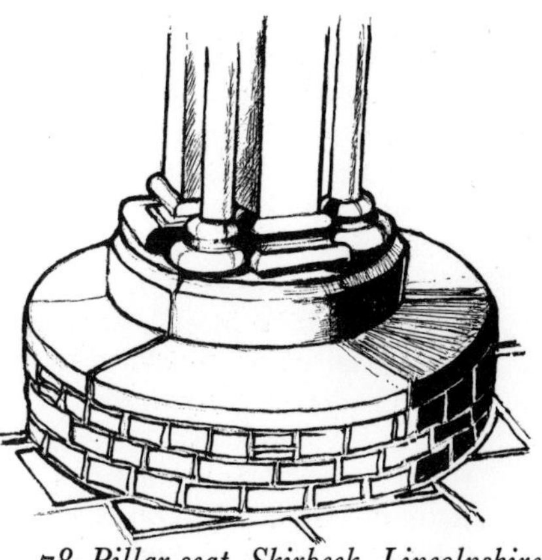

78 Pillar seat, Skirbeck, Lincolnshire
thirteenth century

century, and the bases often had an extra projection which could serve as a seat such as at Skirbeck, Lincolnshire (*78*).

Doorways were generally pointed, as at Uffington, Berkshire, or trefoiled as at St Cross, Hampshire (*67*). The recessed orders are either left plain or enriched with dog-tooth and stiff-leaf ornament.

A small *priest's doorway*, on the south side, leading directly to the chancel, became a common feature during the Early English period. A most attractive example is at St Mary's Higham Ferrers, Northamptonshire, having a trefoiled arch with a rose carved in each cusp.

Doors were frequently large and often double, divided by a slender shaft. A fine example is the west door of Higham Ferrers (*72*). Ironwork was used with great skill. The south door of Eaton Bray has three hinges on which is displayed some of the most perfect scroll work of Thomas of Leighton, one of the master smiths of the thirteenth century (*68*). His work is also seen on the west door of Leighton Buzzard Church. Other fine examples are at St Guthlac's Market Deeping, Lincolnshire, and Worksop, Nottinghamshire.

The **dripstone**, which forms a projecting arch round the outside of doors and windows, throws off rain and thus protects the mouldings beneath from weathering, is generally clearly marked and frequently terminates in a *corbel* either side of the arch, usually carved in the form of a head or a floral motif. An example is at St Cross, Hampshire (*67*).

The **porch** was now a recognised feature of church building and was used for both religious and secular purposes. In the porch the first part of the sacrament of baptism and the marriage ceremony was performed; also the transaction of legal business relating to parish affairs. Early English porches vary in design, the more usual type projecting boldly beneath a steep pitched gable, as at Barnack, where the south porch is one of the finest in England. It is high pitched and has a vaulted roof covered with heavy stones. The west porch at Higham Ferrers is extremely rich, the whole wall surface being covered with sculpture and a surface decoration composed of square or lozenge shapes, called *diaper work*.

The early phase of the Early English style is characterised by the excessively tall and narrow lancet headed **windows**. These windows were at first single lights, as in the north transept of Chipstead, Surrey (*79*), and Headington, Oxfordshire, but later were arranged in groups of *three*, as at St Mary's Witney, Oxfordshire and St Mary le Wigford, Lincolnshire (*83*); *five* as at Holy Trinity Bosham, Sussex, and St Peter's Oundle, Northamptonshire (*81*); and *seven* as in the east window at St Mary and All Saints Ockham, Surrey. In the north and south walls of the chancel at St Andrew's Cherry Hinton, Cambridgeshire *c.* 1120, pairs of lancet windows are ranged in a continuous arcading richly moulded and supported by slender shafts. Towards the middle of the thirteenth century groups of lancet windows were surmounted by a

79 Lancet window, north transept Chipstead, Surrey, thirteenth century

80 Stone, Kent, c. *1240*

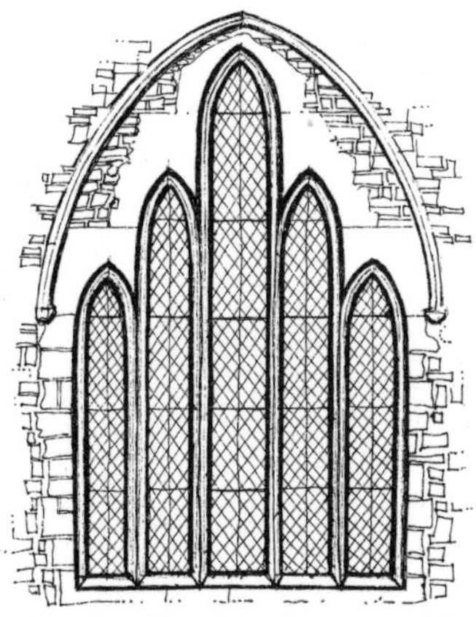

81 Oundle, Northamptonshire c. *1200*

82 Charlton on Otmoor Oxfordshire, c. *1240*

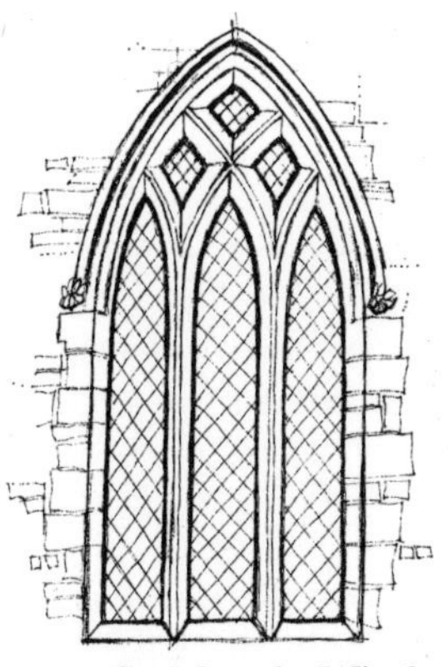

83 St Mary le Wigford Lincoln, c. *1260*

84 East window Raunds, Northamptonshire, c. *1260*

dripstone. In the space at the head of the windows so grouped, simple circles, or openings of trefoil or quatrefoil were pierced. This is called *plate tracery*. Examples are at Barton Stacey, Northamptonshire, Irham, Lincolnshire, Charlton on Otmoor, Oxfordshire (*82*), Little Wenham, Suffolk, Berden, Essex, and Raunds, Northamptonshire (*84*).

Window arches are richly moulded inside and outside with a particularly wide splay inside, often decorated with shafts and delicate mouldings. A fine example is at Stone in Kent (*80*). Circular windows were sometimes constructed in the gables of churches as at Calbourne, Isle of Wight. In some of the smaller churches square-headed windows are seen, as in the chancel at Cowley, Oxfordshire, Tixover, Rutland, and the tower of Ringstead, Northamptonshire.

Niches were common in which sculptured statues were placed.

In Early English work a greater variety of west fronts is displayed than in any other style, the most frequent treatment being three or more lancet lights with a small window above them in the gable, as at Strixton, Northamptonshire.

Early in the thirteenth century a **piscina** niche was constructed in the eastern jamb of the window to the south of the high altar and by the end of the century double piscinas were common as Pope Innocent I stated it to be unseemly that the priest's hands should be washed in the same basin as the sacred vessels. Among the many attractive double piscinas surviving are those at Polebrooke, Northamptonshire, Cowling, Suffolk, and Pulham St Mary, Norfolk (*87*). Trefoil arches with dog-tooth mouldings over the piscina heads are seen at East Dereham, Norfolk. This type of ornamentation is particularly common in Cambridgeshire, as at Cherry Hinton. It was usual to see a stone or wooden shelf near the head of the piscina on which to place the cruets containing the water and wine, and the box of wafers. Where the wooden shelf has been destroyed, the grooves remain.

Fine examples of **sedilia** can be seen at Uffington, Berkshire, Rushden, Northamptonshire (*88*), Adderbury, Oxfordshire, and Stepney in the East End of London. The arches over the latter spring from paired shafts.

Paintings on **interior walls** became more elaborate and depicted gospel stories, as at West Chiltington, Sussex, Wimborne, Dorset, Dauntsey, Wiltshire, and Easby in Yorkshire.

Of **crypts** built during the thirteenth century, a small one of two bays lies beneath the west end of the nave of St Olave's Fenchurch, London, and beneath the south porch at Saffron Walden, Essex.

Fonts were invariably octagonal and raised on a stepped platform; the earliest known is at Charlton, Oxfordshire. Fewer fonts survive showing Early English characteristics than any other styles. The font at Hexham, Northumberland (*70*), decorated with dog-tooth is, however, a good example. Patrington, Yorkshire, has a twelve-sided font, and

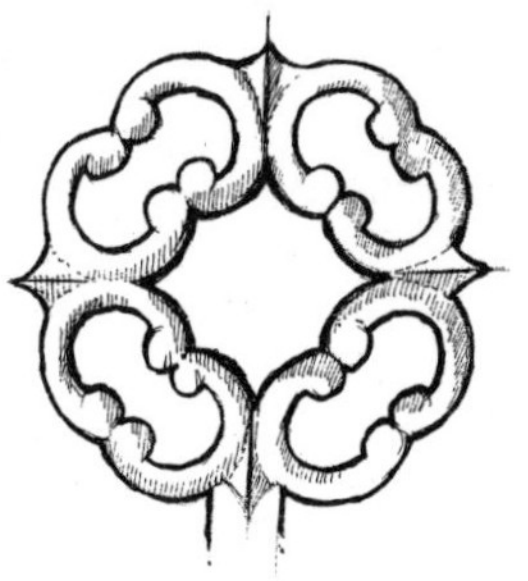

86 Gable cross
Morton, Lincolnshire

85 Broach spire on
thirteenth-century tower
St Mary's Stamford, Lincolnshire

87 Piscina, Pulham St Mary, Norfolk
late thirteenth century

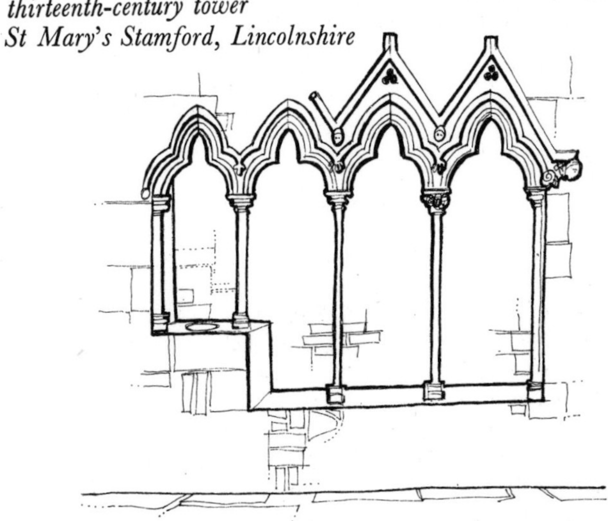

88 Sedilia and piscina, Rushden, Northamptonshire

fonts cast in lead can be seen at Frampton, Siston, Oxenhall and Tidenham in Gloucestershire.

Recumbent effigies were first used on **tombs** during the thirteenth century and are clad in priestly vestments or knightly armour. The tomb of Robert de Vere, fifth Earl of Oxford *c.* 1296 is worthy of notice. This is at St Andrew's Earls Colne, Essex, and is richly ornamented with sculpture and figures in niches along the side of the tomb.

Brass memorial slabs also made their first appearance in England at this time; the earliest known, at Stoke d'Abernon, Surrey, dates from 1277.

Decorated 1300–1350

This is the richest period of Gothic architecture and, as its name implies, it is elaborate in decoration. In many small parishes, however, the window tracery is its most distinguishing feature.

To meet the needs of the growing population in the larger towns and villages, the parish church **plan** was one of continuous expansion: lengthways by the elongation of nave and sanctuary, and laterally by the addition of aisles and transepts which were used as chapels. The plan in general was an aisled nave with a western tower, an unaisled chancel and a north and south porch of which Boston, Lincolnshire, and Warmington, Northamptonshire, are typical examples. A perfect achievement of a new church building completed during the Decorated period is that of Heckington, Lincolnshire. **Triforia** diminished to make room for taller clerestories and to give a more lofty nave arch, taller piers, higher roofs and larger aisle windows.

In the existing churches numerous varieties of plan occur. The addition of an aisle or aisles was the most common form of expansion as this could be achieved with the minimum amount of inconvenience. To the twelfth-century church of St Luke Stoke Hammond, Buckinghamshire, transepts were added with a central tower, and the chancel was rebuilt; a new cruciform church was founded at Poynings, Sussex *c.* 1370, and the church of St Thomas Simpson, Buckinghamshire, was rebuilt. The aisled cruciform plan reached its highest expression in the rebuilt and larger churches of St Mary Melton Mowbray, Leicestershire, St Mary Redcliffe, Bristol, and St Patrick Patrington in the East Riding of Yorkshire (*89* and *90*). In these three churches the transepts have the unique feature of east and west aisles. At All Saints Shillington, Bedfordshire, aisles were added to the nave and chancel, and to the cruciform plan, such as that of Castor, Northamptonshire, aisles were constructed to extend flush with the end walls of the transepts. Both

89 Patrington, Yorkshire fourteenth century

90 Plan of Patrington

these extensions formed an aisled rectangle which became a favoured plan during the second half of the fourteenth century, and was widely adopted in East Anglia and in the south-west of England.

The foundation of **guilds' chapels** increased throughout the country and side by side with them grew up the **chantry chapels** donated by wealthy benefactors of the parish where prayers could be said for their well-being in life and for the repose of their souls after death. Four such chapels flank the south aisle of the nave of St Mary's Scarborough, Yorkshire.

With the more general availability of **stained glass** came the desire to increase the number and size of the windows in proportion to the stone **wall** surface. In order to achieve this lighter construction **buttresses** were formed of great projection and diagonally placed corner buttresses became characteristic of the Decorated period. *Flying buttresses* were constructed to span externally over the aisle roof.

Buttresses all vary in design and in degree of ornament. At Beaulieu, Hampshire *c.* 1300, can be seen plain buttresses which terminate in a slope under the cornice; at St Mary's Bridlington, Yorkshire *c.* 1300 they run through the battlement and have decorated triangular heads (*109*). An example of buttresses with niches and carved clumps of foliage, called *crockets*, over the canopies, can be seen at St Mary's Great Milton Oxfordshire *c.* 1320 (*110*).

Timber **roofs** still prevail in the majority of parish churches and are covered by tiles, lead, or wood shingles. Although mainly in the larger parish churches, a general elaboration of stone vaulting is characteristic of this period, leading to intricate star and web patterns with natural foliage *bosses* carved at the rib intersections.

Timber roofs of distinctly Decorated style, as at Dunsfold, Surrey, Adderbury Oxfordshire, Wysall, Nottinghamshire, and Raunds, Northamptonshire (*108*), are rare. An example of a tie beam construction is at Brenchley, Kent *c.* 1350 where it is used in conjunction with trussed rafters. A trussed rafter roof is preserved at St Mary's Dennington, Suffolk, and an arch braced roof in the naves of St Margaret's Starston, and St Mary's Middleton, Norfolk.

During the fourteenth century the art of building tall, elegant and finely proportioned **spires** reached fruition. Many new ones were erected and many spires were added to existing **towers** and an excellent combination is the spire of St Mary Stamford, Lincolnshire, where the Early English tower is finished with a fourteenth-century spire (*85*). The broach spire was abandoned in favour of a more slender and graceful form springing from within the tower parapet, and crockets and pinnacles became features of tower and spire design. Broaches were, however, used in conjunction with angle pinnacles in the spires of Grantham, Lincolnshire and Newark, Nottinghamshire. Flying buttresses were used to give greater stability and were set from pinnacles at the angles of the tower to the canted sides of the spire, as can be seen at St Andrew's Whittlesey, Cambridgeshire.

Gable crosses are not common, but a fine example survives at Haslingfield, Cambridgeshire (*107*).

Spire lights were frequently used in this period, examples being seen in the Northamptonshire churches of Polebrooke and St Katherine Irchester.

Stair lights in towers were generally long narrow slits, usually ornamented with foliation or tracery such as at St Mary's Beverley, Yorkshire *c.* 1350. In the belfry small unglazed openings called *sound holes* were introduced during the fourteenth century, as at St Michael's Alderbury, Shropshire, and Great Addington, Northamptonshire *c.* 1350 (*99*). The name 'sound hole' is inappropriate as they were more strictly ventilation holes to give air in the ringing loft.

Tower windows were frequently partially filled with stonework as at St Michael's Aynhoe, Northamptonshire *c.* 1350. At All Saints Irthingborough, Northamptonshire *c.* 1350 they are constructed as two single lights divided by a niche containing a statue (*96*).

Piers were often of a diamond shape formed with clustered shafts set close together with fillet moulding or small hollows between each shaft. Sometimes they have a central shaft with four attached shafts, being divided by deep hollows, as at St Denis's Silk Willoughby, Lincolnshire. In small churches the multi-angular flat-faced pier is common, as at St Peter and St Paul's Long Compton, Warwickshire (*104* and *105*), and Chacombe, Northamptonshire.

Capitals are of infinite variety, being moulded or carved with naturalistic foliage as at Patrington (*102* and *103*).

Bases tend to become taller and are set on octagonal plinths. The early triple roll-moulding is later replaced by ogee mouldings.

The sizes of **doorways** vary considerably. A large single door with side shafts is more common than the double door of the Early English period. Shafts are generally not free standing, but are cut on the jambstone, giving an appearance of lightness, as at St Mary's North Mimms, Hertfordshire. Small doorways are plain and often without shafts, their arch moulding continuing to the ground on either side, as at St Peter and St Paul's Kislingbury, Northamptonshire (*95*), and Brampton, Oxfordshire. In some cases the *dripstone* is the only form of decoration.

The heads of doorways are often double-curved or *ogee* shaped and the tympanum is filled with carved naturalistic foliage or sculptured figures. At Little Addington, Northamptonshire (*94*) an ogee canopy is surmounted by crockets with finials either side.

At Christ Church York *c.* 1320, niches are carved on either side of the door. Earlier **doors** were designed with elaborate applied ornamental ironwork which was gradually superseded by tracery carved in the woodwork, with ironwork confined to the hinges, handles, knockers

91 Stone chancel screen Stebbing, Essex, c. *1340–50*

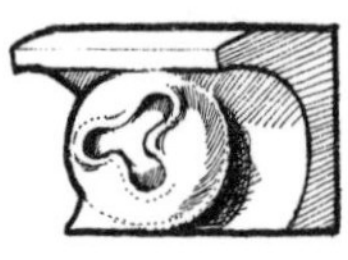

92 Detail of ball flower

93 Detail of four-leaved flower

95 Doorway, Kislingbury, Northamptonshire, c. *1320*

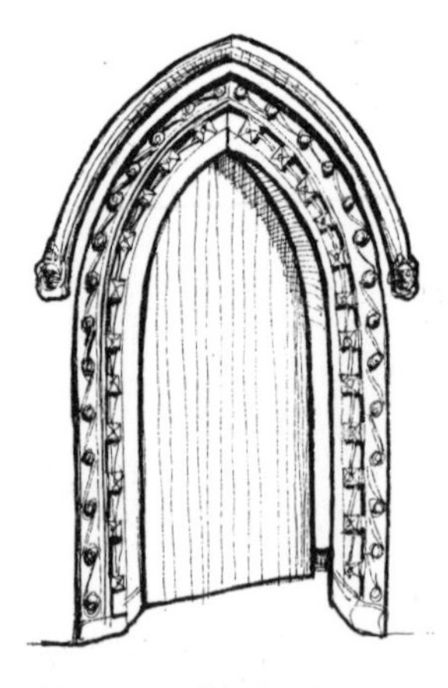

94 Doorway Little Addington, Northamptonshire, c. *1350*

96 Belfry window
Irthlingborough
Northamptonshire, c. *1320*

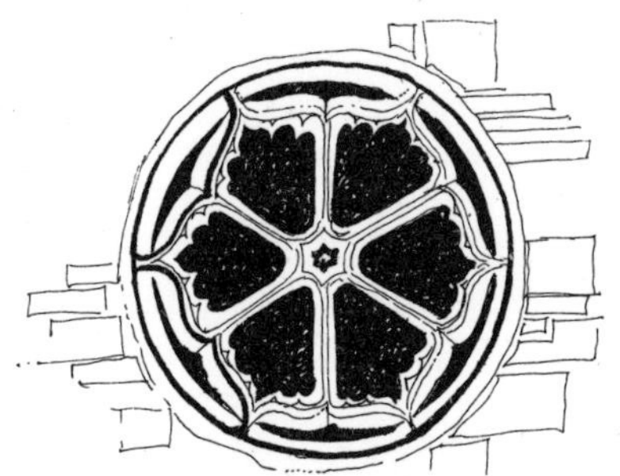

97 Circular window
Stratford on Avon
Warwickshire, c. *1350*

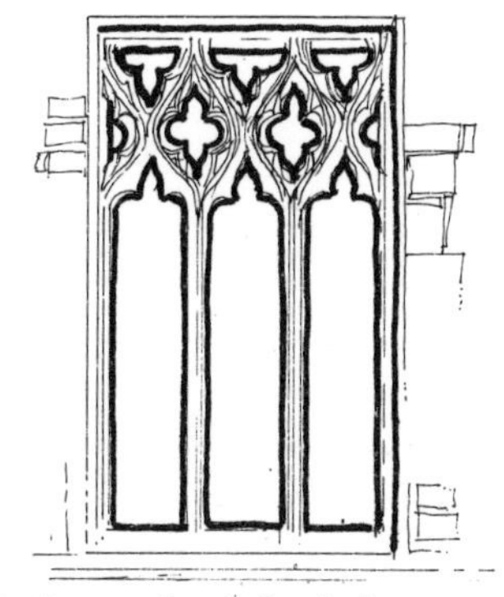

98 Square headed window
Dorchester, Oxfordshire, c. *1350*

99 Belfry window
Great Addington
Northamptonshire, c. *1350*

100 Kent tracery, Chartham, Kent, c. *1280*

101 Ducklington, Oxfordshire

and latches. The door of the south porch of St Lawrence Harpley, Norfolk, St Mary's Swineshead, Lincolnshire, and Meare, Somerset (*106*) are fine examples. The upper part of the vestry door at St Cuthbert's Halsall, Lancashire, is a carved wooden imitation of a five-lights window with flowing tracery, and at Castor, Northamptonshire, the south door has an ornamental border carved with a Latin inscription.

From the fourteenth century onwards it became the practice to build **porches** with upper rooms, of which examples can be seen at St John the Baptist's Thaxted, Essex, and St Nicholas's King's Lynn, Norfolk. These upper rooms were used for the safe keeping of parish records and documents, or for parochial meetings.

The treatment of **window tracery** is the most marked characteristic of the Decorated period. Window arches are divided by one or two mullions branching into flowing *bar tracery* of endless variation. Fine examples of early work are at Munslow, Shropshire, and Eling, Hampshire, and of later work in the north transept of Huish Episcopi, Somerset, Winchelsea, Sussex, Leominster, Herefordshire, Crick, Northamptonshire, and Ducklington, Oxfordshire (*101*).

A particular form of tracery known as *Kent tracery* was developed; a typical example is seen at St Mary's Chartham, Kent *c.* 1280 (*100*), but it is also found in other counties, as at Ayot and Walden in Hertfordshire and Sandiacre and Chaddesden in Derbyshire.

Circular or wheel windows are more common than in earlier periods and examples are seen at St Mary's Cheltenham, Gloucestershire *c.* 1350, Holy Trinity Stratford on Avon, Warwickshire *c.* 1350 (*97*), and Ferrington St John, Norfolk *c.* 1320. Square headed window openings are seen at Dorchester, Oxfordshire (*98*), and Over in Cambridgeshire.

Clerestory windows in the smaller parish church were still often little more than trefoil or quatrefoil openings pierced in the wall. Inside they were generally deeply and widely splayed, as at Cranford St Andrew, Northamptonshire *c.* 1320, and Great Milton, Oxfordshire *c.* 1300.

In the aisled rectangular plan the chancel arch was no longer a structural necessity. The **rood screen** became a prominent feature. Stone was used in the earliest form of rood screen and those at St Mary's Bramford, Suffolk, and St Mary's Welsh Newton, Herefordshire, consist of three open arches carried on columns. A solid base surmounted by traceried panels can be seen at Broughton, Oxfordshire; each panel has an ogee arched head with crockets and finials. A most beautiful and elegant stone screen can be seen at St Mary's Stebbing, Essex, where it is treated as a large traceried window of three lights (*91*).

From the middle of the fourteenth century the rood screen was invariably made of oak. An interesting screen is at St Nicholas's Rodmersham, Kent, where Spanish walnut is used. A substantial beam, constructed above the screen in many churches to take the weight of the rood, is preserved at Tunstead, Norfolk.

102 Capital, Patrington, Yorkshire

104 Capital, Long Compton Warwickshire, c. *1350*

103 Section of pier, Patrington

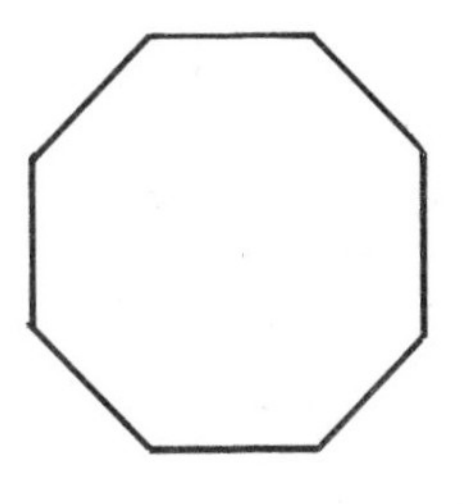

105 Section of pier, Long Compton

106 Detail of ironwork hinge on south door Meare, Somerset, early fourteenth century

107 Gable cross Haslingfield, Cambridgeshire

The **sedilia** and **piscina** are at their richest during this period. The double piscina reverted to a single drain, as it was now the custom for the celebrant of the Mass to drink the ablutions.

Examples of sedilia and piscina as a combined unit are at Swavesey, Cambridgeshire, and Grafton Underwood, Northamptonshire (*115*). Elaborately enriched treatment is given to the sedilia at Hawton, Nottinghamshire, and Heckington, Lincolnshire, and to the piscina at Milton Keynes, Buckinghamshire, and Fyfield, Berkshire (*114*).

By the fourteenth century the ceremony of the Easter Sepulchre was an accepted ritual. It took the form of a liturgical drama symbolising the entombment and Resurrection of Jesus Christ. The **Easter Sepulchre** in its early form was a movable piece of furniture draped with hangings over a timber framework. Later, stone Sepulchres were specifically built, usually on the north side of the chancel, to enshrine the Blessed Sacrament during the Easter Festival. They were of elaborate design and that at Heckington, Lincolnshire, is extremely rich in ornament. At Hawton, Nottinghamshire, the Easter Sepulchre is about 12 ft high. The canopy is carved with foliage and figured sculpture relief. Its ornamental treatment is the finest of its kind in the country.

Interiors of walls were painted with scriptural themes such as the Life of St Mary, and the Last Supper, at Croughton, Northamptonshire. Paintings of the saints survive at St Mary's Chalgrove and All Saints Shorthampton, Oxfordshire. A fourteenth-century painting and colour work was uncovered in 1947 at St Andrew's Pickworth, Lincolnshire.

The *ball flower* (*92*) is a characteristic ornament of the Decorated period and it is used abundantly on the mouldings of arches at St Michael's Ledbury, Herefordshire. Other examples are Heckington, Patrington and Hawton; also at Nantwich, Cheshire and Wick, Northamptonshire.

Flat *four-leafed flowers* (*93*) were popular as a diaper pattern.

Although not numerous, many splendid **fonts** of the Decorated period have been preserved. Examples are at St Peter's, Northampton, and Bloxham, Oxfordshire (*112*).

Tombs are decorated with stone canopies richly carved. The effigies of this period are in a prone position and have carved figures of angels at their heads and dogs at their feet. The sides were frequently panelled and carved with rich heraldic crests. A fine example is the tomb of Sir William de la Pole in Trinity Church, Hull, Yorkshire; also of elaborate design is that of Stephen Alard, a warden of the Cinque Ports, in Winchelsea Parish Church, Sussex (*111*).

The earliest surviving **pulpits** *c.* 1380, are of stone, displaying cusped panelling of the Decorated period, as at Long Coombe, Oxfordshire (*113*), and Nantwich, Cheshire. Pulpit canopies, also of stone, survive in Arundel, Sussex, and Cold Aston, Gloucestershire.

108 Roof construction of nave Raunds, Northamptonshire

109 Buttress, Bridlington, Yorkshire, c. 1300

110 Buttress, Great Milton, Oxfordshire, c. 1320

111 Tomb of Stephen Alard, a Warden of the Cinque Ports, Winchelsea, Kent, Sussex, early fourteenth century

112 Font, Bloxham, Oxfordshire, c. *1350*

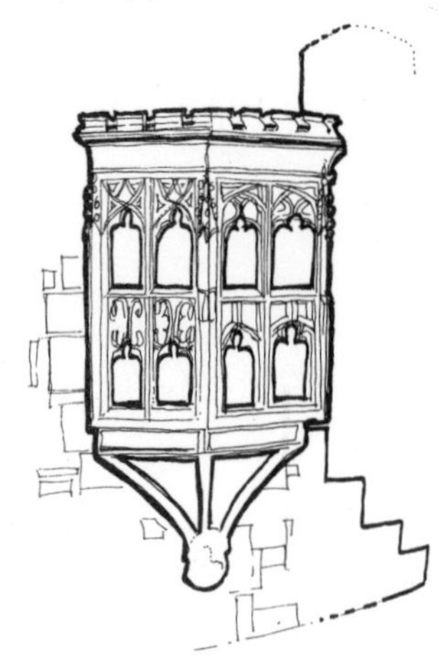

113 Stone pulpit, Long Combe
Oxfordshire
late fourteenth century

114 Piscina, Fyfield, Berkshire, c. *1300*

115 Sedilia and piscina
Grafton Underwood
Northamptonshire, c. *1350*

The oldest extant example of a single desk wooden **lectern** is at Bury, Huntingdonshire.

The period of Decorated Gothic was ended by the Black Death epidemic in 1348, to which about a third of the population fell victims. Many churches were left incomplete and it was not for some twenty-five years that parish church building recommenced.

Perpendicular 1350–1660

In contrast to the ornate work of the Decorated period there evolved the Perpendicular Gothic, an architectural style of purely English creation. It was first employed by the monks in the construction of Gloucester Cathedral—work on which continued uninterrupted by the Black Death. By the middle of the fourteenth century the majority of parishes possessed their own churches, so few new ones were necessary. However, with the growing economic prosperity which came largely from the flourishing wool trade, especially in East Anglia and Somerset, some of the largest and most beautiful buildings, known as *Wool* churches, were commissioned. A great deal of alteration to and enlargement of existing buildings was also carried out.

Outstanding examples of the many splendid *Wool* churches are at Lavenham, Suffolk, Cromer, Norfolk, and Yeovil, Somerset. The latter is sometimes known as the 'lantern of the west' on account of the large number and size of its windows. Holy Trinity Long Melford, Suffolk, also a *Wool* church, is one of the finest parish churches of the fifteenth century (*116* and *117*). The unique feature of a Lady Chapel at its east end makes it without parallel in parish church planning.

The diversity of **plan** and construction was due mainly to the financial resources available. The Perpendicular, however, is a style of spaciousness and of lightness of structure, and is seen at its best in the larger churches. Aisles were added where this had not previously been done, and the aisled rectangle became the general plan; St Nicholas's King's Lynn (*118*) is a clear example. The construction of a clerestory was a common feature and the consequent lowering of the aisle roof. In many cases the triforium was omitted and the clerestory windows were made larger. Clerestories were often divided from the nave by a band of carved decoration or panelling. One of the finest examples of this can be seen at St Mary's Redcliffe, Bristol. Abundant use of panelling is seen during this period, when it was applied to any flat surface.

An aisleless nave and chancel plan with a west tower is seen at St Edmund's Maids Moreton, Buckinghamshire *c.* 1450, and of an un-aisled cruciform plan is St Kenelm's Minster Lovell, Oxfordshire *c.* 1420.

116 Long Melford, Suffolk, late fifteenth century

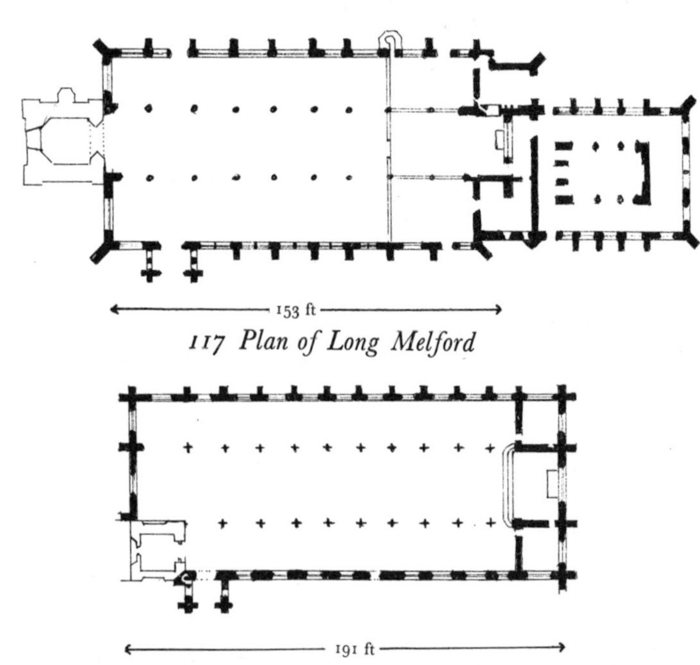

117 Plan of Long Melford

118 Plan of St Nicholas's, King's Lynn, Norfolk

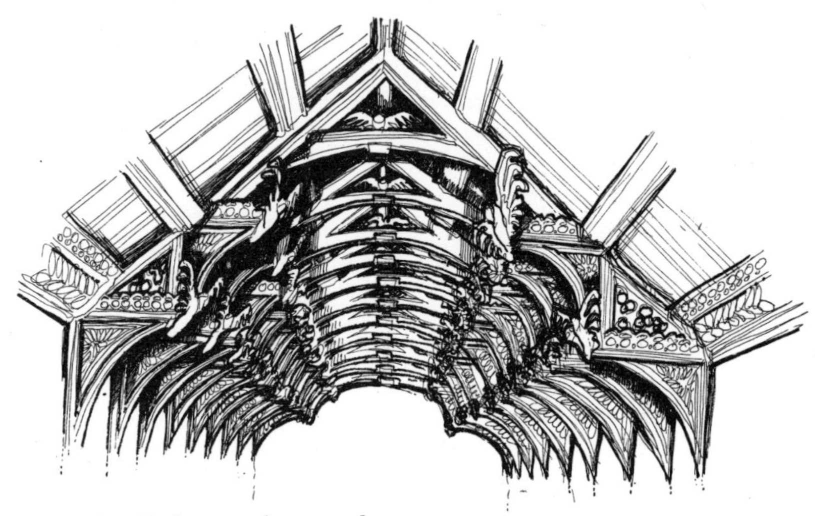

119 Double hammer beam roof March, Cambridgeshire, c. 1500

121 Flying buttress Fotheringhay Northamptonshire

120 Buttress, South Moreton Berkshire

122 Panelled buttress St Laurence, Evesham Worcestershire

The fifteenth century was the golden age for **stained glass** and the Perpendicular style was designed to make the most and best use of it. The increased size of the windows and their form of construction made it possible to reduce the **wall** area to a minimum. Holy Trinity Stratford on Avon, Warwickshire *c.* 1490, presents an example of window space predominating over wall area. The sturdy stone mullions running from sill to head, and the introduction of transoms running horizontally forming large rectangles, greatly offset the lack of wall area which was supported by slender **buttresses** of great projection as at South Moreton, Berkshire(*120*). They were often panelled as at Evesham, Worcestershire(*122*), and terminated with pinnacles rising above the parapet. *Flying buttresses* were in common use to give added support externally between aisle and nave roofs, an excellent example is at Fotheringhay, Northamptonshire(*121*).

Many earlier **roofs** were destroyed when clerestories were built. Open timber roofs of all types are seen during the Perpendicular period, and the most striking development in timber work is the appearance of the hammer-beam roof(*192*) which achieved its greatest popularity by the end of the fourteenth century, and reached its peak in East Anglia in the form of a double hammer beam, as at St Paul's Knapton, Norfolk, and St Wendreda's March, Cambridgeshire *c.* 1500(*119*). Shallow pitched roofs were of tie beam construction supported by richly carved brackets each side. Externally roofs were masked by battlemented parapets.

These open timber roofs were of elaborate construction, often with carved figures of angels. At St John the Baptist's Bere Regis, Dorset, there are twelve projecting figures facing downwards which, it is suggested, represent the twelve apostles.

In the west of England curved trussed rafters are common. These are often boarded on the underside forming a wagon ceiling(*191*) divided into numerous square panels enriched with carved bosses and exquisitely coloured. St Andrew's Cullompton in Devonshire is a very fine example; also Shepton Mallet in Somerset.

Occasionally stone *fan vaulting*(*189*) was used and fine examples can be seen in the aisles at Cullompton and Ottery St Mary, Devonshire (added in 1520), and All Saints Evesham, Worcestershire.

Fan vaulting was also often used in the construction of **porches** which, by the fifteenth century, became small architectural masterpieces. Examples can be seen at Burford, Oxfordshire, Maids Moreton, Buckinghamshire, Spalding, Lincolnshire, and Bodmin, Cornwall.

Gable crosses are less frequently seen. Trunch, Norfolk, however, provides a good example(*128*).

The fifteenth century was very much a **tower** building period, the greatest perfection being reached in Somerset. The tower of St Mary Magdalen's Taunton, is a masterpiece of construction(*123*). Rising to

124 Detail of the 'Boston Stump', Lincolnshire late fourteenth century

123 Tower, Taunton, Somerset c. *1500 (rebuilt 1862)*

125 Typical spike on tower Aldenham, Hertfordshire

a height of 163½ ft it is divided into three stages, the string courses being decorated with quatrefoils. Its right-angled buttresses, decorated with niches and pinnacles, are of small projection in proportion to its height. The parapet is surmounted by bold panelled and battlemented pinnacles, with gargoyles beneath. Each stage has two large three-light window openings, all with a variation of window heads.

Pierced stone battlements are generally a feature of the belfry stage.

Other particularly elaborate Somerset towers are at Blagdon, Wrington, Staple Fitzpaine, Huish Episcopi and Bishops Lydeard.

'Sound holes' or tower lights are more frequently used in the Perpendicular style than in the Decorated, although the tracery is often so much of the flowing character that at first sight would appear to be Decorated work. In many cases it is only by the type of moulding that the date can be established. The tower light at Cromer, Norfolk is a typical example (*134*).

In most towers the stairway is contained within the inner part of the tower. At Evercreech, Somerset, however, this is marked by an octagonal corner projection. Occasionally towers are crowned with spires, as at Louth, Lincolnshire, and Kings Sutton, Northamptonshire.

The famous octagon tower of Ely Cathedral proved an inspiration to masons, and square towers with octagonal lanterns began to appear. Outstanding examples are the towers of St Botolph's Boston, Lincolnshire, known as the 'Boston Stump', rising to 302 ft and the highest in England (*124*), and Lowick and Fotheringhay, Northamptonshire.

The fourteenth-century towers of Ashwell and Baldock, Hertfordshire, have a recessed octagonal storey crowned with a thin spire, little more than a spike. The spike, often rising direct from the tower, as at Aldenham, Hertfordshire (*125*), is a peculiarity of Hertfordshire.

Much tower design was, however, of simple construction with no ornamentation, of which St Michael's Pitsea, Essex, and St Michael's Hawkshead, Lancashire, are typical examples: likewise many of the parapeted towers of Devon and Cornwall.

An elaborate example of a flint tower is at St Peter Mancroft, Norwich, which was completed in 1455. Fine examples are also at Eye, Saxmundham, Southwold and Long Melford, all in Suffolk.

Piers are more slender and frequently octagonal, but with considerable variations of mouldings. Clustered piers, as at St Mary's Beddington, Surrey, have shallower mouldings than in previous periods. At Northleach and Chipping Campden in Gloucestershire, and Handborough, Oxfordshire, the piers of the nave arcade have eight concave sides.

Capitals are plain and are enriched with graceful formalised foliage or figures, generally of angels, shallower in relief than in the Decorated period. In some cases, especially in Devonshire, the capitals are continued round the whole cluster of shafts as at Wolborough (*127*) and

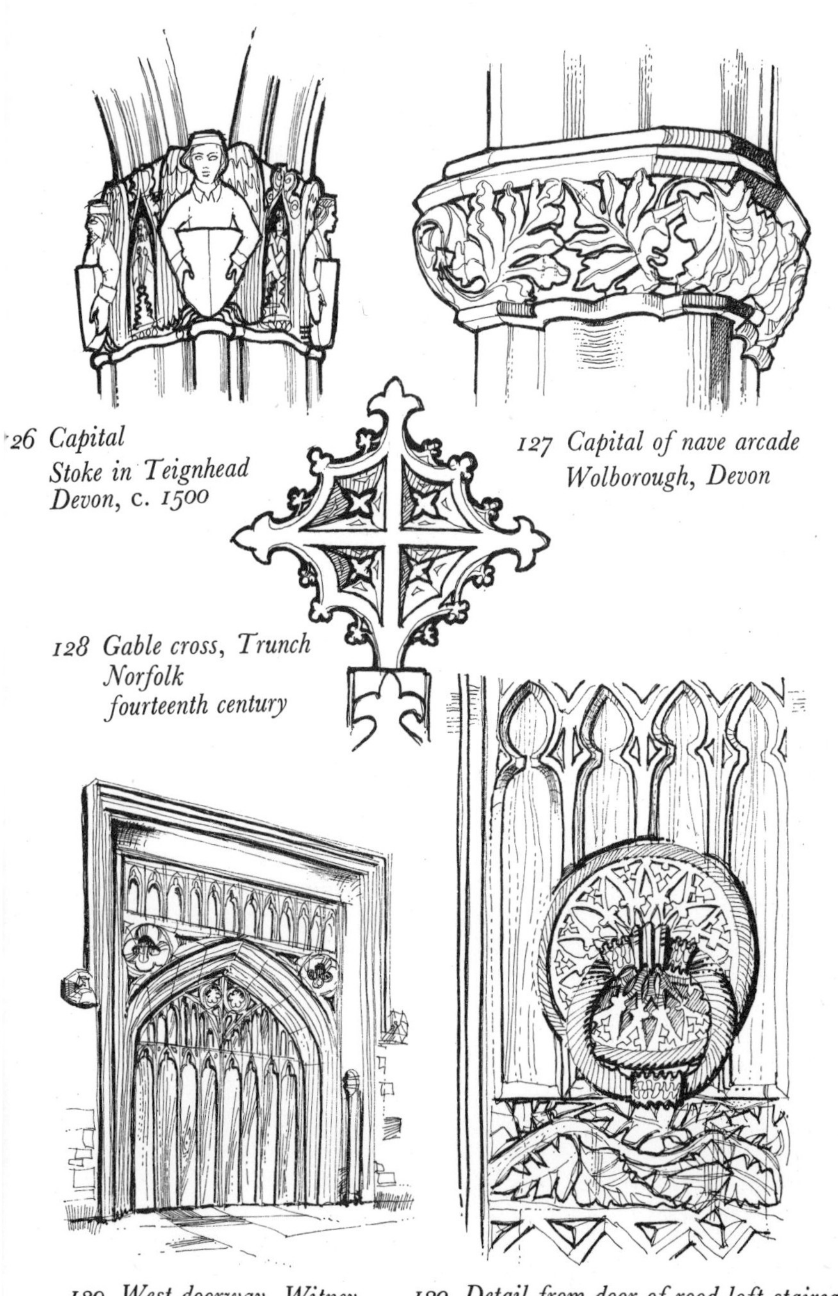

26 Capital
Stoke in Teignhead
Devon, c. *1500*

127 Capital of nave arcade
Wolborough, Devon

128 Gable cross, Trunch
Norfolk
fourteenth century

129 West doorway, Witney
Oxfordshire

130 Detail from door of rood loft staircase
Stogumber, Somerset

Stoke in Teignhead (*126*). Frequently capitals are omitted altogether, as at St Peter and St Paul's Ormskirk, Lancashire, and St Fimbar's Fowey, Cornwall, where the mouldings of the nave piers are carried straight up into the arches.

The plinths of the **bases** are of slight projection, octagonal or polygonal in form. They can be distinguished from the Decorated by their greater height and frequent use of ogee mouldings.

The distinctive feature of Perpendicular **doorways** is the square hood mould or dripstone over a four-centred arch. The triangular spaces between the dripstone and arch were often carved with a coat of arms. The jambs are frequently ornamented with slender shafts with plain capitals. Their high octagonal bases, in common with plinths generally, show ogee moulding. Examples are at Warkton, Northamptonshire, Kenton, Devonshire, and the west doorway of Witney, Oxfordshire (*129*).

Doors were frequently panelled with Perpendicular tracery and examples survive at Thurlton, Norfolk, Helmingham, Suffolk, and Stogumber, Somerset (*130*). The south door at Martham, Norfolk, has a fine carved border of grapes and vine leaves, and at St Giles's Balderton, Nottinghamshire, the door is carved with an inscription. Ironwork was used only for hinges, handles and latches.

The flowing curvilinear window tracery of the Decorated period gave way to perpendicular mullions running from sill to head. From these perpendicular mullions, which are a distinctive feature of this period, is derived the term *Perpendicular* referring to the whole period.

The upper portion of many **windows** is divided into a series of panel-like compartments such as the east window of St Margaret's Lowestoft, Suffolk, Swinbrook, Oxfordshire (*131*), and Leigh, Lancashire (*133*). The large window of eleven lights, filled with innumerable rectilinear panels at St Nicholas's King's Lynn, Norfolk, is a fine example of Perpendicular work. The cusps of the tracery grow more naturally out of the mullions than in earlier work.

Where an ogee shaped dripstone is used over either door or window, it is often decorated with crockets, as at Rushden, Northamptonshire (*135*).

Windows in the south and west aisles of Denford, Northamptonshire, though on first sight they appear to be Decorated, are indeed late Perpendicular, when there was a partial return to the previous style (*132*). In the south transept of St Peter's Lowick, Northamptonshire, double transoms can be seen. Square-headed windows are less common, but an example is at St John the Baptist's Tideswell, Derbyshire, where the large chancel *c.* 1380 is lighted by square-headed windows of three lights.

There was of course a period of transition and, especially in East Anglia, Decorated forms of windows are found side by side with the

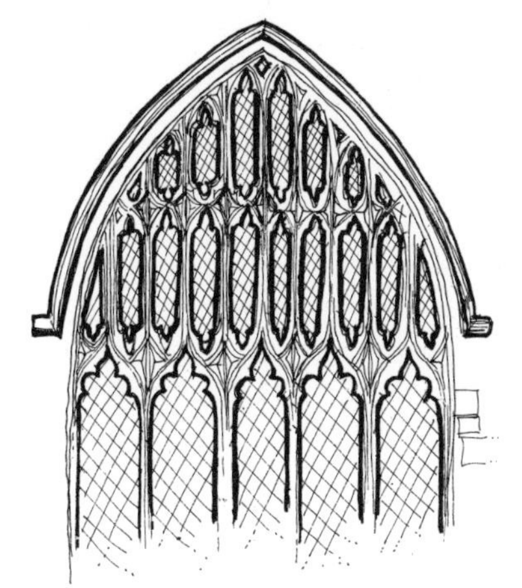

131 Swinbrook, Oxfordshire, c. *1500*

132 West window of south aisle Denford, Northamptonshire

133 Leigh, Lancashire

134 Tower light, Cromer Norfolk

135 East window, Rushden Northamptonshire

Perpendicular style. The fine east windows of St Andrew's Soham, and St Andrew's Sutton, Cambridgeshire, show the beginning of Perpendicular tracery.

Stained glass windows of special interest still survive at St Mary's Fairford, Gloucestershire 1493, which is one of the last churches to be built before the Reformation.

The **low side window** in the chancel is frequently seen.

By the Perpendicular period the **rood screen** had replaced the chancel arch and afforded the opportunity for elaborate wood carving. The beam that supported the rood remains intact at Denston, Suffolk, and at Cullompton, Devonshire.

The late fifteenth-century stone screen at St Swithin's Compton Bassett, Wiltshire, has a front arcade of three four-centred arches, behind which is an openwork screen, the two being joined by a panelled vault. Stone screens such as at St Mary's Totnes *c.* 1460 and St Michael's Awliscombe, Devonshire, have the qualities of timber design.

Chantry chapels are divided from the nave by **parclose screens** found chiefly in East Anglia and of exceptional design are those at Dennington, Suffolk.

One of the numerous and varied **sedilia** of fifteenth-century workmanship is at Great Gransden, Huntingdonshire, where grooves are clearly seen for the insertion of a wooden shelf. Another example is at St Mary's Adderbury, Oxfordshire.

A jamb **piscina** of the fifteenth century at St Mary's Cheltenham, is surmounted by battlements and sculptured figures. A fine example of a piscina incorporated in the design of the sedilia is at Tilney All Saints Norfolk(*136*).

Interiors of walls continue to be painted, as at Pickering, Yorkshire, Breage, Cornwall, Penn, Buckinghamshire, and South Leigh, Oxfordshire. There is a famous Doom painting at St Peter's Wenhaston, Suffolk *c.* 1480, and the largest now remaining in England is at St Thomas's Salisbury. This was painted when the clerestory was added and the wall above the chancel arch raised.

Fonts are generally supported by angels and raised on steps. They are commonly panelled, each panel being filled with sculpture. Fine ones at Trunch, Norfolk and St Peter Mancroft, Norwich are now much mutilated. Those known as the Seven Sacrament fonts were found in Norfolk and Suffolk towards the end of the fifteenth century and fine examples survive at Walsoken, Sall, Syleham and East Dereham(*137*).

Wood carving was at its greatest perfection in the fifteenth century and **font canopies** of wood were elaborately carved. Ufford, Suffolk, and Halifax, Yorkshire(*138*) provide excellent examples. That at St Peter's Offord d'Arcy, Huntingdonshire, is four times the height of the font.

Until the fourteenth century, when fixed **seats** were introduced, it

136 Sedilia and piscina
Tilney All Saints, Norfolk

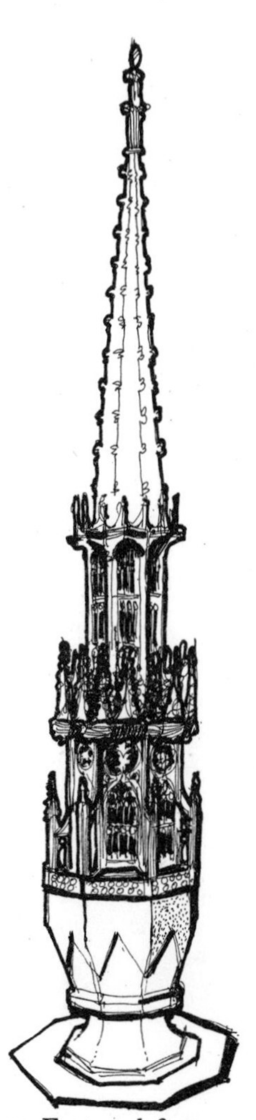

137 Font and font cover
Halifax, Yorkshire

138 Seven-sacrament font
East Dereham, Norfolk, c. *1468*

was the custom for the congregation to kneel or stand. Earlier than this there had been a few stone seats against the walls in some churches or, in some cases, the bases of piers had an extra projection which could serve as a seat, as at Sutton Bonnington, Nottinghamshire, and Skirbeck, Lincolnshire(*78*). The earliest fourteenth-century example of fixed benches is at Clapton in Gordano, Somerset, but the ancient pews at Dunsfold, Surrey, are reputed to date from the end of the thirteenth century. Early benches have plain solid ends, but later in the period bench ends were beautifully carved as at Brent Knoll, Somerset, Dennington, Suffolk and Wiggenhall St Mary the Virgin, Norfolk.

Pulpits were commonly made of oak and, although all have had some form of restoration, about 100 survive today. Those exhibiting the richest carving are in Devonshire, as at Kenton, Haberton and East Allington. Biblical scenes, the saints and clerical divines were often painted in colour on the panels. The peak of this form of additional decoration was reached in East Anglia and examples can be seen at Southwold, Suffolk, and Burnham Norton, Norfolk.

Stone pulpits are octagonal in shape with Perpendicular tracery. There is a delightful group in the north-east of Somerset, all of about 1480, of which Banwell and Worle are the richest; also some ten in Devonshire, of which South Moulton would appear to be the earliest.

One of the most striking **lecterns** of the early fifteenth century is a wooden eagle at the church of Astbury, Cheshire. The more usual design is desk-shaped, or double desk-shaped, as at Romsey, Hampshire *c.* 1450. An example of a bronze eagle lectern is at St Mary's Wiggenhall, Norfolk 1518.

Tombs received a less rigid treatment. A knight and his wife were laid side by side, their hands clasped. Pillows were carved at their heads with ministering angels or cherubs, and lap dogs at their feet. The alabaster effigies at Lowick, Northamptonshire 1419, are fine examples.

The Reformation

By the Act of Supremacy 1535, Henry VIII declared himself Supreme Head of the Church in England, over which he exercised dictatorial powers. Confirmed by the Six Articles of Religion of 1539 he was determined to uphold the Catholic Faith in everything save the supremacy of the Pope and, apart from the adoption of the Tyndale and Coverdale translations of the Bible, the Catholic liturgy and rites were wholly maintained throughout his reign. With the advent of the rule of the Protector Somerset came the wholesale destruction of ecclesiastical buildings in an outward show of protest at the corruption within the Church. The monasteries and chantries had already been suppressed during the reign of Henry VIII and now the parish church at the height of its greatness suffered immeasureably in a wave of iconoclasm which swept away any 'superstitious' object. Practically all church building was brought to a standstill. In 1550 the stone altars were ordered to be replaced by holy tables of wood, set in a convenient place in the chancel. Mary Tudor's legislation to restore communion with Rome and the rites and furnishing of the Catholic Faith led at her death to further spoliation. The situation was saved by Elizabeth I, who re-established the independence of the Church in England with herself as Supreme Governor, and by the Act of Uniformity in 1559, re-introduced the Prayer Book of 1552 without the addition of extreme Protestantism, and declared the Church in England to be Catholic but Reformed.

The Elizabethan period was one of comparative inactivity as far as the parish church is concerned. Sufficient churches had been built during the previous centuries to meet the needs of the population and the majority of these were in a deplorable condition through having suffered the ravages of the Reformer. Repairs and rebuilding were slow to take effect and what new churches were built reflected little the impact of the Italian Renaissance which was then revolutionising architectural Europe (although this impact *was* felt in domestic work).

Among the parish churches built during the Elizabethan period are the little brick church of St Michael Woodham Walter, Essex 1563, with its crow-stepped Tudor gables (*139*), St Mary's Watton, Yorkshire *c.* 1550, with square-headed window openings and Easton Royal, Wiltshire 1591. An unusual example of Elizabethan building is the seven-sided porch at Sunningwell, Berkshire.

An exceptional instance of rebuilding during this period is at St Michael's Framlingham, Suffolk. Here, *c.* 1549, Thomas Howard, third Duke of Norfolk, erected a chancel which was almost as large as, and wider than, the nave, to provide a worthy resting place for the 'Norfolk' family.

In the tombs of this period is seen the influence of the Dutch, Flemish and German artists and craftsmen who came to England during the Renaissance. From the prone position of previous centuries the figures are now depicted kneeling, their hands in prayer, as on the famous Culpepper tomb at Goudhurst, Kent. Other tombs where this influence can be seen are those of John Harrington (*d.* 1524) at St Peter and St Paul's Exton, Rutland, Thomas Cave (*d.* 1558) at St Nicholas's Stanford, Northamptonshire; also the terra-cotta monument to Henry Lord Marney (*d.* 1523) in Layer Marney Church, Essex.

By order of Queen Elizabeth I in 1560 the Ten Commandments and the Lord's Prayer were to be lettered on either side of the royal arms under the chancel arch and these now occupied the place of the rood. An example of this is seen at Baddiley Cheshire(*140*). It is, however, interesting to note that according to churchwardens' accounts prior to 1560, this had already been done in many churches. The earliest known instance is at St Michael's Worcester 1547.

With the consequential liturgical reform which began to take place after the 1559 Act of Uniformity, the spiritual barrier between clergy and laity was broken. From being merely present at the services which were conducted in Latin and which they could not understand, being cut off from the chancel by the rood screen so that they could not see, the laity were now encouraged to participate in services in their own language. Under the influence of William Laud, when he was made Bishop of London in 1628, a new impetus was given to church building, mainly in the form of alteration. Adapting existing buildings caused many difficulties, for although the removal of the chancel screen was relatively simple, the chancel was often so long that the priest was inaudible. To overcome this problem, in many parishes, specific parts of the church were used for corporate worship; the chancel and sanctuary for Holy Communion, the nave for mattins and evensong, and the side chapels for weekday services. The adoption of this idea did much to prolong the Gothic style.

During the seventeenth century another onslaught was made on any 'superstitious' object, this time by the *Puritans* who caused untold damage by their wholesale destruction to crucifixes, images and paintings.

The position and meaning attached to the altar or holy table was still under heated discussion and in 1643 the House of the Lords and Commons issued an Ordinance for the demolition of all stone altars, and for the removal of all holy tables from the east to a convenient place in the chancel or body of the church.

The Puritans whitewashed over all paintings on the walls and no colour was allowed except on the royal arms.

139 Woodham Walter, Essex

140 Tympanum dividing chancel from nave,
Baddiley, Cheshire
The lettered Creed, Commandments, Lord's Prayer
and Coat of Arms are dated 1663

The few new churches built after 1600 were of a simple plan, and have no chancel. Examples of these are St John's Groombridge, Kent 1625, St Katherine Cree, London 1628, St John's Leeds 1631, and St Mary's Leighton Bromswold, Huntingdonshire *c.* 1634.

The Civil War of 1642–50 was to cause yet further destruction to the parish churches and many were in effect turned into Presbyterian chapels or closed altogether. Plaxtol, Kent, and Holy Trinity Berwick on Tweed, Northumberland 1652, were two of the few churches to be built during the Commonwealth of 1642–60. As Archbishop of Canterbury William Laud decreed in 1645 that all altars or holy tables should be replaced at the east end of the church, and in order to restore reverence for the sanctuary he was instrumental in reintroducing altar rails, thus emphasising its separateness from the chancel. The use of altar rails had been adopted in Elizabethan times, but these were removed by the Puritans. An exceptionally fine example of Laudian altar rails is at Wormleighton, Warwickshire.

The Mediaeval Church

Since the Reformation the mediaeval parish church had lost much of its original purpose; the altar-house had become a preaching room suited to the needs of the Reformed liturgy.

After 1700 box pews replaced the benches, except at the back of the church where in country districts space was reserved for shepherds and their dogs. Galleries were constructed where necessary to give additional seating accommodation.

Plaster ceilings were very much in fashion for domestic buildings, and even the old churches with finely carved and decorated roofs were given plaster ceilings in both nave and chancel.

A **three-decker pulpit** was often placed in the centre of the nave obscuring the view of the altar from the congregation. At the bottom sat the clerk who read the notices and led the responses. From the centre the priest conducted the main part of the service, and preached from the top deck.

If not already appearing under the chancel arch, the Lord's Prayer and the Ten Commandments were often lettered in gold on black boards placed on either side of the altar in the sanctuary.

The fourteenth-century church of St Thomas of Canterbury, Fairfield, Kent, was remodelled in the eighteenth century and it still contains the box pews, text boards and a three-decker pulpit of that date; the twelfth-century church of St Mary Whitby, Yorkshire, was similarly reconstructed.

Renaissance Architecture

The inspiration for European architecture originated in Greece. The spacing and dimensions of three variations of column, each with its distinctive entablature over the columns, make up the Three Orders of Greek architecture known as *Doric*, *Ionic* and *Corinthian* (*141*). The Romans adapted these pure designs and added two further Orders: the *Tuscan*, which is a variation of the Doric (*141*), and the *Composite*, a mixture of both Ionic and Corinthian (*141*). The entablature consists of an architrave, frieze and cornice.

The rediscovery in 1414 of a treatise on the classical architecture of Ancient Rome, written in 23 BC by Vitruvius, a Roman architect and surveyor, led to a Classical Revival in architecture based on his plans of the structure of the temples of Ancient Rome.

Andrea Palladio and his followers were the chief exponents of the Renaissance form in Italy and in the late sixteenth century Palladio made a thorough study of Vitruvius's manuscripts and detailed records of the classical architecture of Rome. In 1570 he published *I quattro libri dell' Architectura—The Four Books of Architecture*—in which the principles of Vitruvius's work are clearly reiterated.

The first classical church to be built in England was St Paul's Covent Garden 1631–8, to the design of Inigo Jones, who had visited Italy and had studied the works of Palladio. The church is planned as a large undivided rectangle based on the plan of a Roman temple. The main façade consists of a wide Tuscan portico and a simple pediment. The church was destroyed by fire in 1795 but stands today reconstructed almost to its original plan.

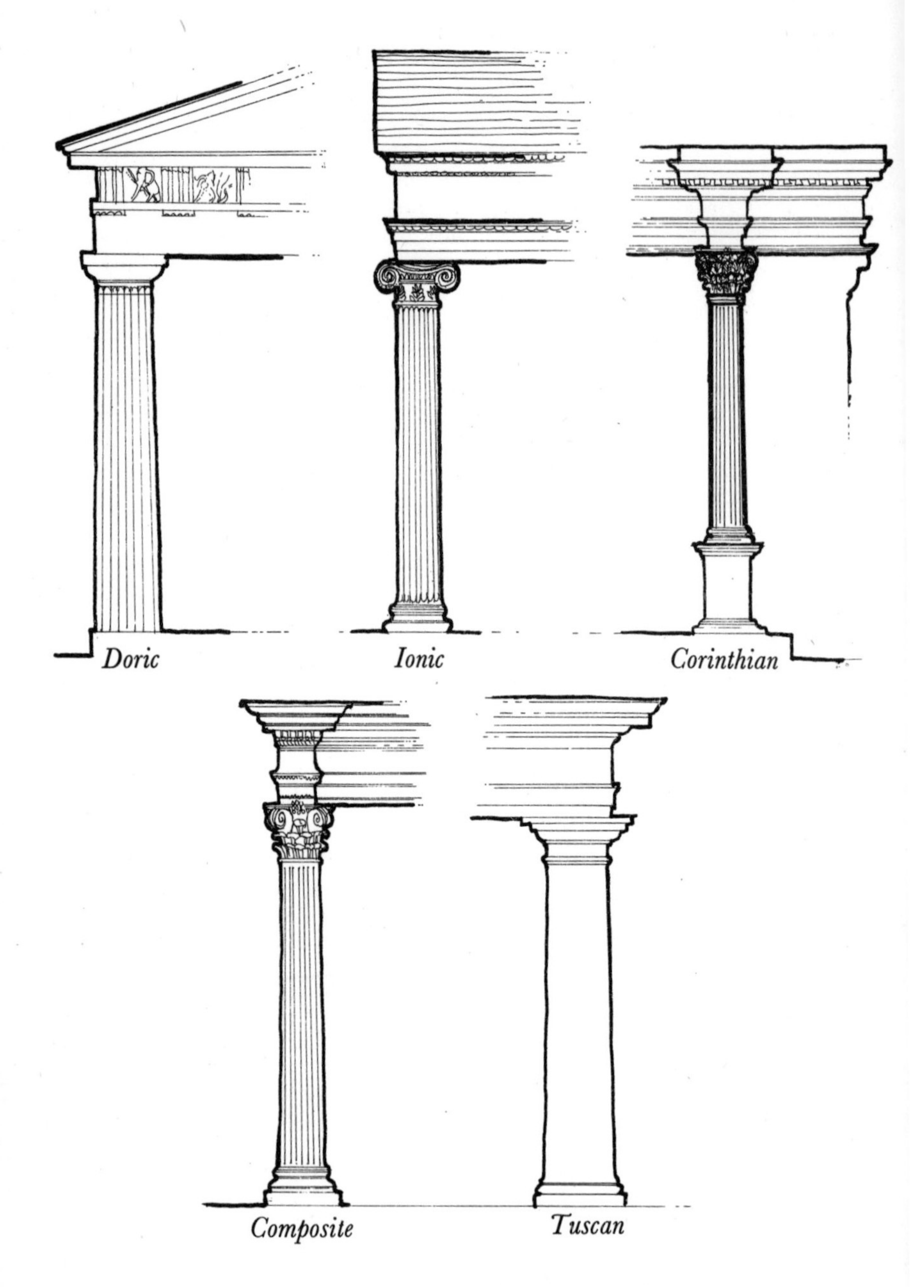

141 The five Orders of Roman architecture

The Classical Age 1660–1830

The Classical Age, beginning with the work of Wren and sometimes referred to as the Pillar and Portico era, can be divided into four periods; their dates inevitably overlapping, and each dominated by the work of an individual architect: The Age of Wren 1669–1721, Baroque 1700–1750, Palladian 1750–1830, and the neo-Greek Revival 1800–1830.

With the Restoration of the Monarchy, political and religious strife lessened, the Anglican rite was restored and Puritanism lost any hold it might have had as a controlling force in the Church of England. A Puritan influence, however, remained within the Anglican Church, keeping an even balance between Anglicanism and Catholicism.

The first phase of church building after the Restoration was the outcome of the Great Fire in 1666, when 87 City churches were destroyed. Gifts of money from individual parishes and private resources were not adequate to meet the heavy cost of rebuilding and even with the additional help of a tax levied by the Government on coal arriving at the Port of London, of necessity a number of parishes had to be united. The reconstruction of 51 City churches, also St James's Piccadilly 1684, and St Clement Danes 1684, in the Strand, both just outside the City boundary, were placed in the hands of Christopher Wren, who in 1669 was appointed Surveyor General to the Royal Works, a position which he was to hold for 50 years.

The Renaissance church was designed as a complete unit to meet the liturgical needs of the newly Established Protestant faith and the auditory plan became accepted in general by all contemporary architects. The **auditory plan** is a single undivided room where the laity can see and hear, and fully participate in all parts of the service. Where necessary, to avoid excessive length, a gallery was constructed on three sides of the building, supported by columns of one of the Orders. The specific development of the auditory plan was a revolution in church design, its fine execution being largely attributable to Sir Christopher Wren, and of which Inigo Jones's design for St Paul's, Covent Garden, is a unique forerunner.

A chancel or screen was occasionally constructed, as at St Paul's Walden, Hertfordshire *c.* 1727, and St Michael's Cornhill 1670–2 in the City of London.

The **walls** are generally constructed of large blocks of ashlar masonry, the angles often rusticated i.e. formed with heavy rectangular blocks of stone to give the appearance of additional strength. Brick was frequently used with quoins laid alternately in brick and stone.

Doorways vary in design from the simple as at St Benet's, Paul's Wharf 1683, to the carved and moulded doorway flanked by columns or pilasters as at St Andrew by the Wardrobe and St Lawrence Jewry* (*149*).

Window openings are fairly large with semi-circular heads and glazed with clear glass, divided into small panes. The use of clear glass predominated over the use of stained glass to provide ample lighting to the church. Fine examples of stained glass, however, can be seen in most of the Wren churches. Sometimes swags of fruit and leaves were carved in stone above the window openings on the exterior walls, as at St Benet's* (*145*) and St Lawrence Jewry* 1671–7. Circular windows are a usual feature, and lunette windows to admit light through the dome, as can be seen at St Stephen Walbrook and St Mary Abchurch* (*146*).

The semi-circular arches of both windows and doorways are generally constructed with promenent key stones, and often rusticated (*148*).

Interiors are lavishly enriched with ornate plasterwork ceilings with relief work radiating from a central device. They are painted in white and gold.

The **woodwork** displays magnificent carvings, frequently of corpulent cherubs, fruit and flowers, emphasising the earthly, as opposed to the spiritual symbolised by the angels and saints of the Gothic age. The richest decoration is usually concentrated in the reredos, and the pulpit.

The most famous wood carver of the day was Grinling Gibbons, whose work is seen in many of the Wren churches. Especially magnificent examples are the reredoses of St James's Piccadilly 1682–4 (*153*) and St Mary Abchurch,* and the pulpits of St Stephen Walbrook (*155*) and St Magnus the Martyr.

Pulpits are of hexagonal shape set on a slender pedestal, reached by a stairway often planned on a graceful curve. A sounding board above, to reinforce the voice of the preacher, lends itself to a wide variety of decoration.

Fonts are generally small with slender pedestals. In St James's Piccadilly is preserved the famous Adam and Eve font carved in alabaster, and at St Margaret Lothbury is another of superb workmanship (*156*), both attributed to Grinling Gibbons.

Tombs and monuments are usually large, showing free standing statuary often in more secular than devotional poses. Semi-reclining figures are frequently seen, as on the Fettisplace monument at Swinbrooke, Oxfordshire. The inclusion of an angel and cherbus in a group is a common feature and the monument to the Duchess of Montague at Warkton, Northamptonshire 1775, is an excellent example. Memorial busts are fashionable, and the monument to Judith Strode at Knebworth, Hertfordshire 1662, with its extremely restrained detail, shows the pure artistry of Italian work.

* are Guild churches which have no parochial functions but are included here to illustrate particular points as architecturally there is no significant difference.

Wren and his followers 1669–1721

Wren handled with ease and assurance the classical forms to suit his own individual designs and brought to maturity the Renaissance architecture of the parish church. His designs varied considerably as they were skilfully adapted to secure the best results from the invariably cramped and irregular-shaped London sites, and the small financial means available. The chief point of planning, Wren records, is to make sure that all can see and hear the preacher of the Gospel, and galleries must be provided if necessary to ensure this rather than to lengthen the church beyond a convenient distance of hearing.

The larger number of Wren's churches are of the single unit auditory plan of which St Edmund the King, St Nicholas Cole Abbey* (restored 1961), and St Michael Paternoster Royal* are still standing. Others have a single aisle, as at St Margaret Lothbury and St Clement Eastcheap; or north and south aisles, as at St Bride's Fleet Street (restored 1958) and St Michael's Cornhill. The most unusual plan of all is Wren's design of a ten-sided oval for St Benet Fink, Threadneedle Street (now destroyed).

Owing to their close proximity to other buildings the exteriors are not very imposing, although where they occupy a prominent site, such as St Lawrence Jewry* (*142*) (restored 1957) and St Benet's, Paul's Wharf* (now used by the Church of Wales), they are most impressive.

Building materials varied. Portland stone was favoured, but as it was expensive, bricks had to be used a great deal, reserving stone for the quoins or corners.

The towers and steeples, each unique in design, present a most remarkable exterior feature with their focal interest on the upper stages which, in the days of Wren, rose above the other nearby buildings. Of exceptional beauty are the Gothic spire of St Dunstan in the East (*152*), and the steeple of St Mary le Bow (*151*) (church restored June 1964) rising in Portland stone from a tall tower with a rusticated Doric doorway decorated with cherubs (*148*). In contrast but none the less effective is the low brick tower of St Benet's, Paul's Wharf.* The tower of St Michael's Cornhill (*150*) added by Nicholas Hawksmoor in 1671, and that of St Mary Aldermary are of the Perpendicular style, their four corners rising to turrets surmounted by finials.

A central dome was an interesting conception of Wren and St Stephen Walbrook 1676 is one of the best parish church examples (*143* and *144*). Although of a simple rectangular plan the church is given a cruciform appearance by the interior arrangement of four groups of four Corinthian columns supporting the 42 ft diameter dome. St Mary at Hill and St Martin Ludgate* are of similar construction.

*are Guild churches which have no parochial functions but are included here to illustrate particular points as architecturally there is no significant difference.

142 St Lawrence Jewry, 1671–7

144 Plan of St Stephen Walbrook

143 St Stephen Walbrook, 1672–9

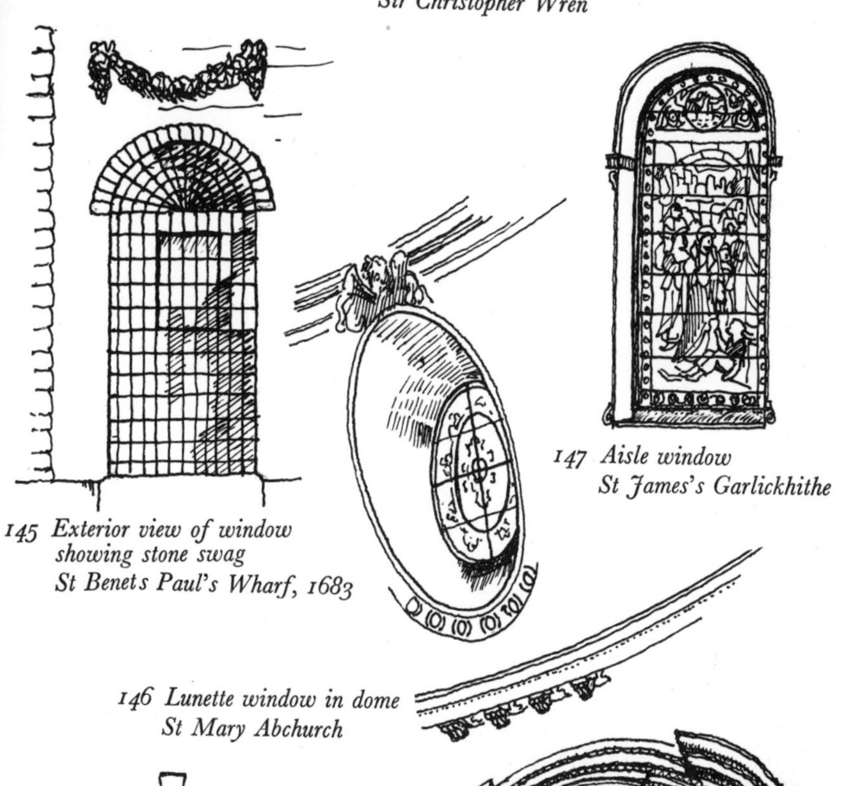

145 Exterior view of window showing stone swag St Benets Paul's Wharf, 1683

146 Lunette window in dome St Mary Abchurch

147 Aisle window St James's Garlickhithe

148 Tower doorway St Mary le Bow, 1670–80

149 Interior doorway St Lawrence Jewry, 1671–7

151 *Steeple, St Mary le Bow*
1670–80

150 *Gothic tower, St Michael Cornhill*
Nicholas Hawksmoor, 1721

152 *Gothic steeple*
St Dunstan in the East, 16

153 *Detail from reredos*
St James's Piccadilly, 1682–4

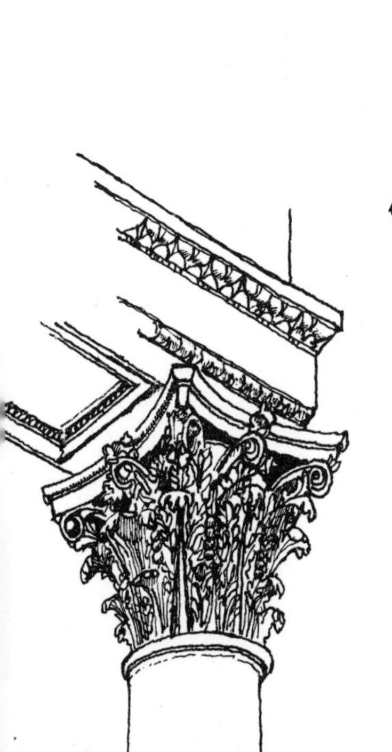

154 *Detail of corinthian column*
St James's Piccadilly
Sir Christopher Wren

155 *Pulpit*
St Stephen Walbrook

Wren was predominantly a London architect. His influence, however, spread far outside the City of London and he did design a few country parish churches, among them St Mary's Ingestre, Staffordshire 1673–7 (*157*) and All Saints Farley, Wiltshire 1690 (*158*). St Mary's has a narrow nave with side aisles. The chancel is divided from the nave by a screen, the nave arcade being composed of semi-circular arches with prominent decorated keystones on piers made up of four three-quarter round Doric columns clustered together.

Wren's influence is seen also in the rebuilt churches of St Peter Gayhurst, Buckinghamshire 1728, St Catherine Wolverton, Hampshire 1717, and St Peter and St Paul Blandford, Dorset 1731–9.

One of Wren's closest associates, Robert Hooke, designed the squat brick church of St Mary Magdalene Willen, Buckinghamshire 1679–80, and Henry Bell, another of his associates, was responsible for the design of All Saints North Runcton, Norfolk, one of the finest eighteenth-century churches in England.

156 Font St Margaret Lothbury

157 *Ingestre, Staffordshire, 1676*

158 *Farley, Wiltshire, 1688–90*

Baroque 1700–1750

By 1700 architects were finding the true Renaissance form a little monotonous and were striving after freedom in design and novelty of treatment. From this reaction arose the new phase in architecture known as the Baroque, easily distinguishable by its massiveness of form, exaggeration of decoration, twisted and rusticated columns and broken pediments. This style, like the Classical, emanated from Rome and quickly spread throughout Europe, each country adapting it to its own national characteristics.

Traces of Baroque can be seen in some of Wren's later churches, such as the spires of St Nicholas Cole Abbey and St Martin's Ludgate, but its chief exponent in the field of parish church architecture is Nicholas Hawksmoor, one of Wren's former pupils. Hawksmoor designed six of the 51 metropolitan churches authorised by the 1711 Act of Parliament and in these he displays remarkable individuality. They are St Alphege's Greenwich 1711, St Anne's Limehouse 1712–24, St George in the East Stepney 1715, St George's Bloomsbury 1720–30 with its pyramidal spire surmounted by a statue of George I (*160*), Christ Church Spitalfields 1725, with its unusual and lofty west steeple and portico (*162*), and St Mary Woolnoth 1716–19, with its fortress-like rusticated façade and curious tower with composite columns surrounded by two low turrets (*159*). St George in the East was destroyed in the bombing of 1941. It is now rebuilt and was dedicated in April 1964. The churches of St Paul Deptford 1712, St Philip Birmingham (now the cathedral) and St John Westminster (gutted 1941), are fine examples of the Baroque style. They were built under the 1711 Act to the designs of Thomas Archer.

An early example of the Baroque tendency is seen in the porch of All Saints Oxford 1707–8, with its twisted columns and broken pediment (*161*). A late example in its most exaggerated form is the interior of St Michael's Great Witley, Worcestershire 1735. The whole of the wall area and ceiling are adorned with baroque plasterwork in white and gold, enriched with painting.

John James's design for St George's Hanover Square 1713–24 is another example of Baroque work. This has a portico of six Corinthian columns and a cupola-capped tower.

The Gothic Survival

Gothic architecture survived to a certain extent throughout the Renaissance period, especially in the country and provincial towns which were not caught up by metropolitan fashion. Sir Christopher Wren was himself responsible for restoring the Gothic churches of St Mary Aldermary and St Sepulchre; also the spire of St Dunstan in the

159 St Mary Woolnoth, 1716–19

160 Spire, St George's Bloomsbury, 1720–30

161 Porch, St Mary's Oxford Nicholas Stone, 1637

162 Portico, Christ Church Spitalfields, 1723–9

East (*152*). However, it is recorded that he used the style in its extreme simplicity and only to meet his clients' wishes.

Palladian 1750–1830

Baroque was never a popular phase in English architecture and soon there was a return to the strict classicism first attempted in England by Inigo Jones (see page 75). This, however, is best displayed in domestic architecture, as the influence of both Wren and James Gibbs continued in the majority of new parish church building.

In the Palladian style Robert Adam designed Gunton, Norfolk 1769, Mistley, Essex, where only the two towers survive, and Binley, Warwickshire 1773 with an elegant octagonal cupola at its west end. The large and splendid church of St Peter and St Leonard Horbury, Yorkshire, designed by John Carr 1791 in a style developed from the Palladian by Robert Adam, has an Ionic south porch with fluted Corinthian arcades, and a three-tiered steeple surmounted by a spire. An imposing church of Classical style is Thomas Hardwick's parish church of St Marylebone, built of Portland stone 1813–17, with a Corinthian portico; also to his design is the church of St Mary the Virgin Wanstead, Essex 1787–90, of brick faced with Portland stone, a Tuscan portico, a cupola and windows at two levels.

The Palladian influence is again seen in the design by John Wood Junior of Bath for St Nicholas Hardenhuish, Wiltshire 1779, with its apsidal sanctuary, balustraded parapets, venetian windows and small domed tower.

James Gibbs 1682–1754

Of outstanding ability and individuality was James Gibbs, who, although working to both the Baroque and Palladian character where his clients insisted, produced designs independent of both schools.

One of his first commissions was the design of St Mary le Strand 1713. In 1721 came that of St Peter's Vere Street, London and, as his masterpiece, the famous parish church of St Martin in the Fields Trafalgar Square 1722 (*163*). Here broad flights of steps lead from three sides to a lofty six-columned Corinthian portico. The interior is of the auditory plan with a gallery on three sides. Tall Corinthian columns support the nave vault, with a rich plasterwork ceiling. Behind the west pediment rises a graceful and well proportioned steeple.

In addition Gibbs was responsible for the design of All Saints Derby (now the cathedral) 1725, incorporating in his design the impressive Perpendicular tower of 1527 which dominates the city.

To Wren's church of St Clement Danes, James Gibbs added the tower (*1819*) from the entablature below the clock upwards. This

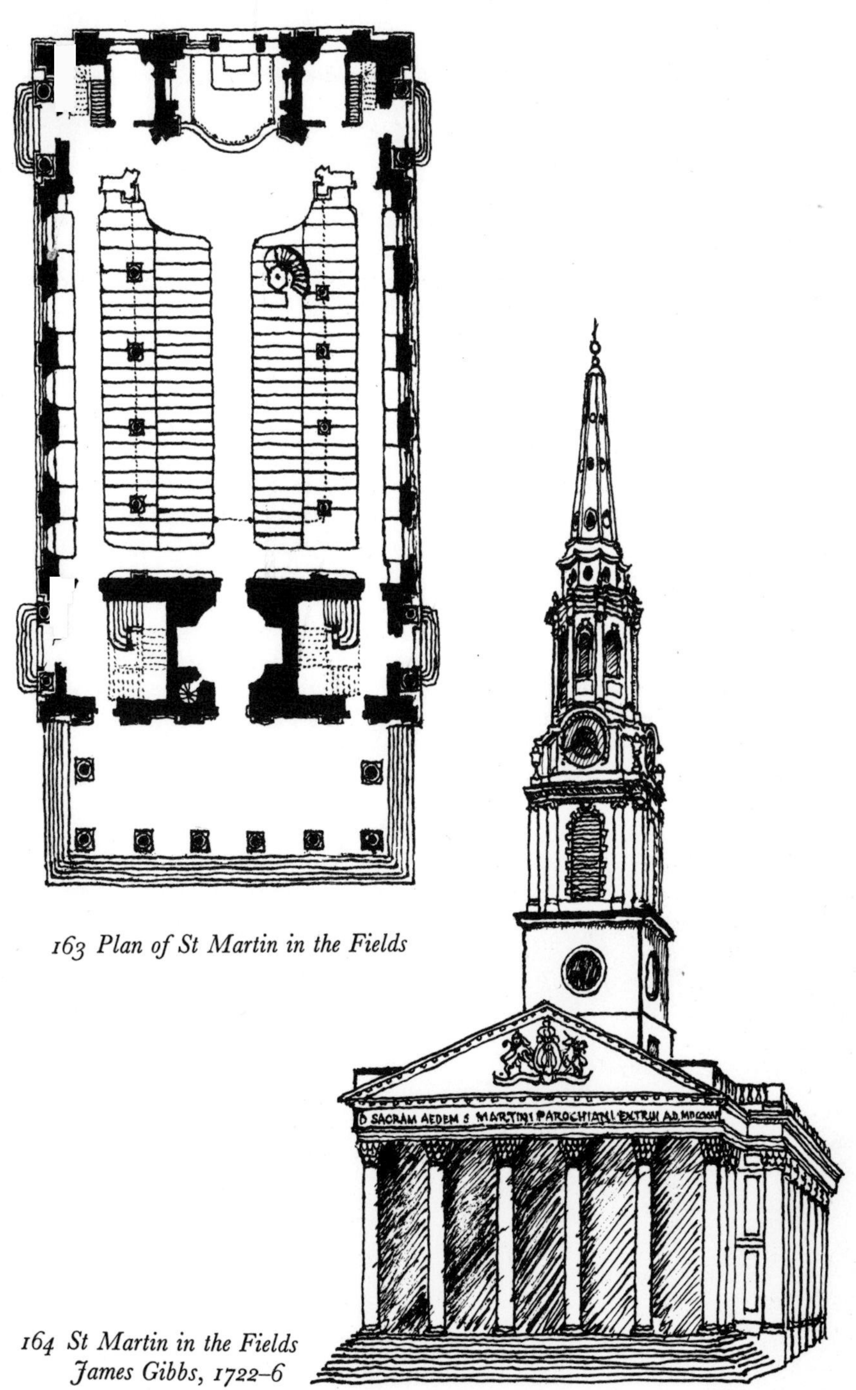

163 Plan of St Martin in the Fields

164 St Martin in the Fields
James Gibbs, 1722–6

church was gutted in 1941, but was restored in 1958 as the RAF church.

The influence of Gibbs's design for St Martin in the Fields can be seen up and down the country as in the church at Mereworth, Kent 1744–6, Holy Cross Daventry, Northamptonshire, and St John's Wolverhampton, Staffordshire 1755–60. Gibbs's alternative plan for a circular building was not carried out, but it was followed by George Steuart in his design for St Chad's Shrewsbury 1790–7, and All Saints Newcastle upon Tyne, of the same date.

Neo-Greek Revival 1800–1830

Towards the end of the eighteenth century two architects, James Stuart and Nicholas Revett, returned from Athens, having made an extensive study of the classical architecture of Greece, and led the way to its revival in England. The church of All Saints Nuneham Courtney, Oxfordshire 1764, with its two Ionic porticos, is to the design of James Stuart. Nicholas Revett is responsible for the design of the church of Ayot St Lawrence, Hertfordshire 1778 (*166*). The columns of the portico are similar to those at the Temple of Apollo at Delos, the remainder of the building being of Palladian style. One of the clearest examples of the neo-Greek revival is the church of St Pancras 1819, designed by W. and H. W. Inwood and based on the Erechtheum in Athens (*167*). A fine example also is John Nash's design for All Souls Langham Place 1822, with its spiked spire and unconventional circular Ionic portico (*165*).

A number of churches were built in the Classical style under the 1818 Church Building Act (see page 92), of which perhaps Sir John Soane's designs for St Peter's Walworth 1824, Holy Trinity Marylebone 1824–5, and St John's Bethnal Green, are the most notable.

166 Plan of Ayot St Lawrence, Hertfordshire
Nicholas Revett, 1778–9

165 All Souls, Langham Place
John Nash, 1822–4

167 St Pancras, London
W. and H. W. Inwood, 1819–22

The Georgian and Victorian Age 1750–1900

Neo-Gothic

A sentimental nostalgia for the past, precipitated in the field of literature, was revived by the Romantic Movement setting a fashion for what is termed neo-Gothic or Gothick. The style is a false and, to a certain extent, frivolous imitation of true Gothic in both materials and methods of construction.

Examples of this work in church building are few. The majority consisted of a decorative superstructure in the Gothic style to an auditory plan with classical fittings. One of the most successful is the slim, elegant Gothic of St Mary's Tetbury, Gloucestershire. This church was reconstructed between 1777 and 1781 by Francis Hiorn, and retains its mediaeval tower. Other examples are St Peter's Galby, Leicestershire 1741, by Wing of Leicester, and St John the Evangelist's Shobdon, Herefordshire 1753.

Gothic Revival

A more serious and scholarly approach to Gothic construction evolved during the early part of the nineteenth century. The Industrial Revolution was in full swing, causing a movement of population to the urban areas where expansion was so rapid that social conditions were appalling and atheism was widespread. In 1818 the Church Building Society was formed and there followed the Church Building Act which granted a million pounds for the construction of 214 churches, the majority to be built in the suburbs of London, and the industrial areas of the Midlands, Lancashire and Yorkshire. These churches were to provide the maximum seating accommodation at the minimum cost. Brick was the cheapest material so by far the greater number of churches were thus constructed. They reflected both their utility and the lack of inspiration. All were of the auditory plan, usually with galleries to provide additional seating. Typical examples are seen at St George's Ramsgate 1825–7, to the design of H. Hemsley, and St Peter's Leeds 1835–41, by R.D. Chantrell. An exception is St Luke's Chelsea 1820–4, which is a more faithful Perpendicular structure, designed in stone by James Savage.

Sir Charles Barry was responsible for some of the best Gothic churches of their kind, such as St Matthew's Campfield, near Manchester, and St Peter's Brighton 1823–8.

In the Early English style, which at this time was less popular than the Perpendicular, is E. Garbett's church of Holy Trinity, Theale, Berkshire, certainly one of the more satisfactory buildings of the period.

In the Perpendicular style, with plaster vaults and cast iron columns, Thomas Rickman designed Christ Church Coventry, and St Peter's Preston, Lancashire. He occasionally used the Decorated style, as seen in St Mary's Birkenhead, and St George's Edgbaston 1819–23.

The predominance of uninspired church building of the previous years was indeed a reflection of the neglected state of the religious life in the community. In recognition of this situation Parliament set up in 1835 an Ecclesiastical Commission to carry out administrative reforms. At the same time the *Oxford*, or *Tractarian Movement* came into being. The aim of this Movement was to re-establish the Church of England as a reformed member of the Catholic Church and thus recapture the spiritual character of the Catholic doctrine and ritual. In the following year 1836, A.W.N. Pugin published his book *Contrasts* in which he illustrates side by side the true Gothic as opposed to the neo-Gothic structures, and puts forward the theory that since Gothic, and in particular the Decorated style, was the product of Christian faith in its purest form in England, it must follow that Gothic is the only true Christian style.

Inaccurate as his theory might be, he had an immense influence upon church architecture. The relevance of Gothic to the Reformed church became generally accepted, and 1839 saw the foundation of the *Ecclesiologists* in Cambridge who were members of the *Camden Society* whose aim it was to study the construction, decoration, and furnishings of the Gothic churches. With the ability to make faithful reproductions of the Decorated style the ecclesiologists became over-enthusiastic and instead of preserving the old churches which by 1840 were falling into decay, they restored them by substituting their structurally correct imitations for the genuine work. To them the alterations and additions made in the previous century were intolerable and wherever possible the offending interior fittings were removed.

With the revival of the Catholic liturgy, the altar was restored to its original place as the focal point of worship. It was laid down by the ecclesiologists that new churches should be similar in plan to the fourteenth century Decorated Gothic with the modifications as set out in the 1662 Prayer Book. As a compromise between Pre-Reformation and Renaissance forms of worship Dr Hook, then Vicar of Leeds, and Dr Jebb, introduced a plan which is still accepted in the Anglican church today. This plan consists of a nave and chancel separated by a screen, or preferably by steps, emphasising their distinct functions. The chancel was to be divided into two parts. One part with facing stalls for the choir, and the other the sanctuary of adequate size for the necessary ritual, divided off by altar rails.

A smaller **pulpit** was constructed on the north side by the chancel steps and a lectern placed on the south side. The **lectern** was either in the shape of a spread-winged eagle, or of a book rest. The congregation were to sit in low pews facing the altar.

Whilst reinstating the importance of the altar and the mystery and dignity of the eucharist, the new plan also enabled the congregation to see and hear, and to participate fully in the services.

Sir Gilbert Scott (1810–1877) was one of the chief exponents of the Gothic Revival in the Victorian era, using the style in its purely imitative form. Among his best known churches are St Giles' Camberwell 1844(*169*), St George's Doncaster 1854, and St Mary Abbots Kensington, rebuilt 1869.

Later in the century architects became more adventurous and adapted the style to their individual characteristics and encouraged a large number of artists and craftsmen to work with them.

William Butterfield (1814–1900) was one of the first architects to use polychromatic work in England. He created a highly ornate effect and a somewhat dazzling spectacle by patterning almost every surface with different colour bricks, mosaics, marble, and alabaster. All Saints Margaret Street, in the West End of London, is one of the best examples of his work(*168*); others are at All Saints Babbacombe, Devonshire, and St Matthias Stoke Newington 1851. The fifteenth-century church of St Mary Ottery St Mary, Devonshire was restored by him in 1850.

George Street (1824–1881) also had a fondness for polychromatic work. He incorporated patterns of different colours in the brickwork of his churches and used lavish interior decorations. Aisles in his designs were reduced to mere passageways. Examples of his work, all richly decorated, are St John's Torquay, Devonshire 1861, St Mary Magdalen Paddington 1868–78, where the crypt is of gold, its ceiling painted blue with gold stars, St Philip and St James's Oxford 1860–1, and St Paul's Herne Hill, London 1858.

John L. Pearson (1817–97) revived the apse in his designs and was keen on the addition of side chapels. Among his many churches are St Augustine's Kilburn, London 1870–80, and St Michael's Croydon, Surrey 1885. The latter is one of his finest churches and is constructed in red brick. The interior has tall slim columns and a stone rib-vaulted roof.

The church of St Mary and St Nicholas Wilton, Wiltshire 1840–5, is exceptional. This was designed by Thomas Wyatt and David Brandon, as a special commission, to the Italian basilican plan with a free standing bell tower, and fitted with mediaeval mosaics and marbles imported from Italy. Also unusual is J. W. Wild's graceful basilica for Christ Church Streatham 1840–2, constructed of yellow brick decorated with patterns in red and white.

168 Detail of mosaic, nave arcade
All Saints Margaret Street, London
William Butterworth, 1850–9

169 St Giles' Camberwell, S.E. London
Sir Gilbert Scott, 1844

Twentieth Century

Of the early twentieth century the most outstanding church design in the neo-Perpendicular style is that of St Mary's Wellingborough, Northamptonshire, by Sir Ninian Comper. This church, built between 1906 and 1932, is an example of the perfect blending of both Gothic and Classical styles, meeting the liturgical needs of the Anglican church. Also of this style is William Tapper's church of the Annunciation Old Quebec Street, London 1913.

In its revolt against the last phase of the Gothic Revival the *Arts and Crafts Movement* which advocated Art for Art's sake, made its mark in new churches, particularly in the fittings and ornaments. The massive and imaginative design by E. S. Prior for St Andrew's Roker, Co. Durham 1906, and A. Randell Wells's church at Kempley, Gloucestershire 1903, are excellent examples. Holy Trinity Chelsea 1890, built in a free Perpendicular style by J. D. Sedding, has been called the 'Cathedral of the Arts and Crafts Movement'.

Of original design is the church of St Thomas Hanwell, Middlesex 1900–20, by Sir Edward Maufe, and Sir Edwin Lutyens's church of St Jude Hampstead, London 1910.

The First World War called a halt for its duration (1914–18) to church building. After the war building prices rose sharply and with the noticeable decline in church-going large buildings were no longer a realistic proposition, and few were constructed. Mention should be made, however, of Sir Giles Gilbert Scott's parish church of Stoke on Trent 1928, St Alban's Golders Green, London 1932, and St Andrew's Luton, Bedfordshire 1932. Also Temple Moore's design for St Wilfrid's Harrogate 1909–14, enlarged by his nephew, Leslie Moore, 1924–8, and Sir Ninian Comper's church of St Philip Cosham, Hampshire 1938.

During the Second World War (1939–45) many churches were destroyed by bombs, especially in the larger towns. Some of these have been rebuilt, some have plans for reconstruction, and the sites of others have been sold to contractors for the erection of secular buildings.

In order to meet the needs of the population in the new towns which have come into being since the end of the War, buildings have been designed to include under one roof, a church, a hall, and various ancillary rooms. Interesting examples are Henry Braddock and D. F. Martin-Smith's plans for Crawley New Town (*177* and *178*) and St Andrew's Sidcup Kent (*180* and *181*): the latter being built in two storeys.

Where financial means are strictly limited, and where social amenities are few, dual purpose buildings have been erected to serve as a place of

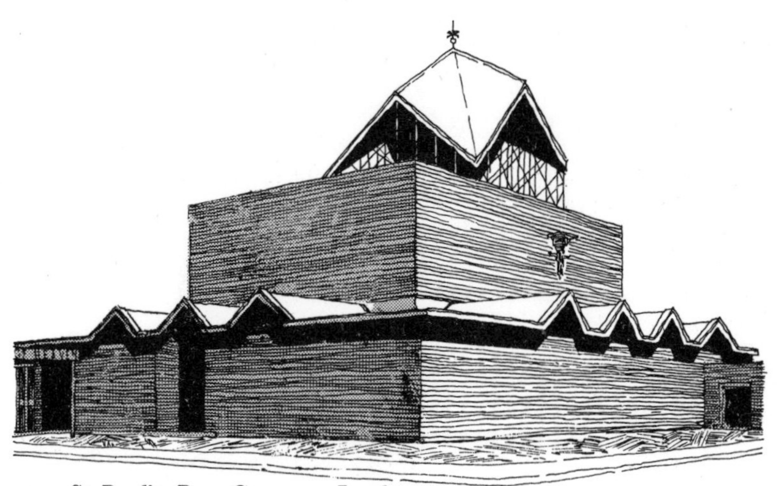

170 St Paul's Bow Common, London
Robert Maguire and Keith Murray, 1960

172 Font and portion of font panel showing sgraffito work
Church of the Epiphany
Merstham, Surrey 1955

171 Section of St Paul's Bow Common

worship on a Sunday and for secular gatherings during weekdays. One such design is St Giles's Bullsover Road, Enfield, Middlesex, by J. Barrington-Barker and Partners 1954. The chapel is separated from the hall by a folding soundproof screen.

The majority of parish churches are still being built to the 'compartmental' plan, but with no structural barrier between nave and chancel, the division being marked by ascending steps. Sir Edward Maufe's church of St Mary Willingdon, Sussex 1953, is based on this plan. Another example is Arthur Bailey's design for the rebuilt church of St Mary Shortlands, Kent 1955(*173* and *174*). St Mary's is constructed of hand-made bricks, with window and door surrounds of Portland stone. Exceptionally large windows with sturdy stone mullions and transoms predominate the wall area to the east and west. A sculpture by John Skeaping of the Flight into Egypt is placed high on the exterior wall of the west front.

The church of the Epiphany on the LCC estate at Merstham, Surrey 1955, is a modern building by Alleyn and Mansel with extensive sgraffito work in the sanctuary, and on a panel behind the font (*172*). This was drawn direct on to the plaster by Theodor Kern. On the exterior south wall there is a sculpture depicting the Epiphany, executed by P. Lindsey Clarke.

The *Liturgical Movement* of today, while acknowledging the altar as the focal point of the church building, emphasises the idea of bringing God to the people as against the mediaeval conception of the people reaching out to God. Experiments are therefore being made with a centrally placed altar, such as St Paul's Bow Common 1960, by Robert Maguire and Keith Murray(*170* and *171*). Here the free standing sanctuary is defined by a large square lantern roof, a 'halo' of metal, and a change in floor texture from precast flags to white flint blocks. Also with a central altar is the church of Holy Trinity, Twydall Green, Kent, by Ansell and Bailey 1964(*175* and *176*). The building is square on plan with a pyramidal roof covered with cedar shingle which contrasts with the rugged surface of the rough brick walls. The main lighting is provided by a large window following the diagonal intersection of the two main roof trusses.

Form follows function, and throughout the ages the plan and structure of the church have been governed by the liturgy of the day. Present day forms are developing as the outcome of modern liturgical outlook, but whatever the style, the parish church of the past, the present, and of the future is built as a living witness to a living God; a place where the Christian community can gather to worship Him, to receive the Sacraments, and to hear His Word.

173 St Mary's Shortlands, Kent
Arthur Bailey, 1955

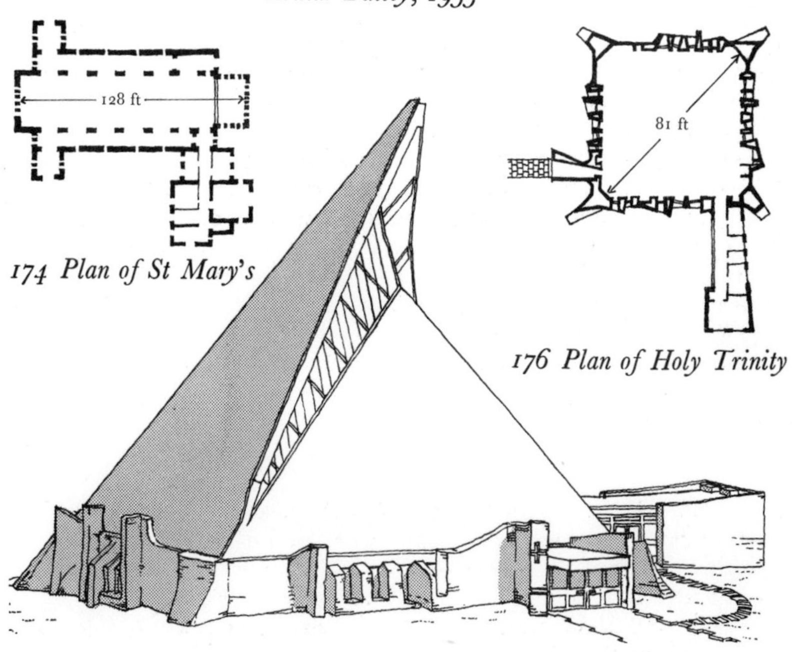

174 Plan of St Mary's

176 Plan of Holy Trinity

175 Holy Trinity Twydall Green, Kent
Ansell and Bailey, 1964

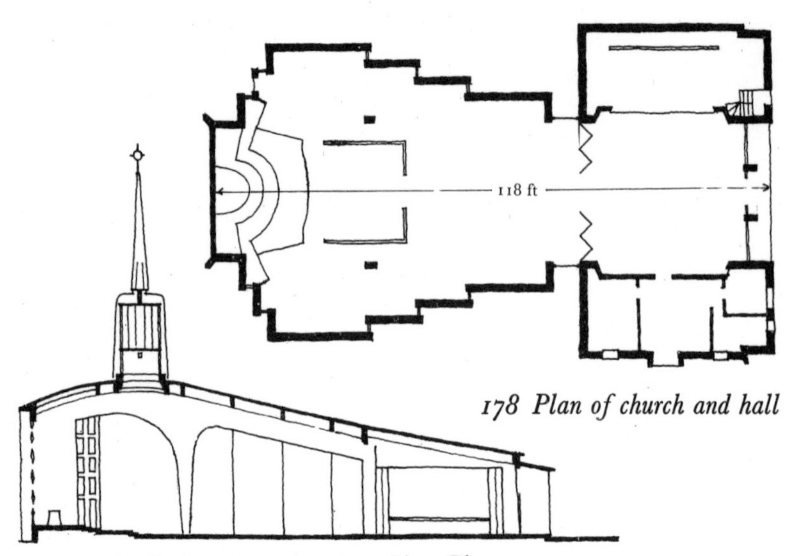

178 Plan of church and hall

177 Longitudinal section, Crawley, New Town
Henry Braddock and D. F. Martin-Smith, 1959

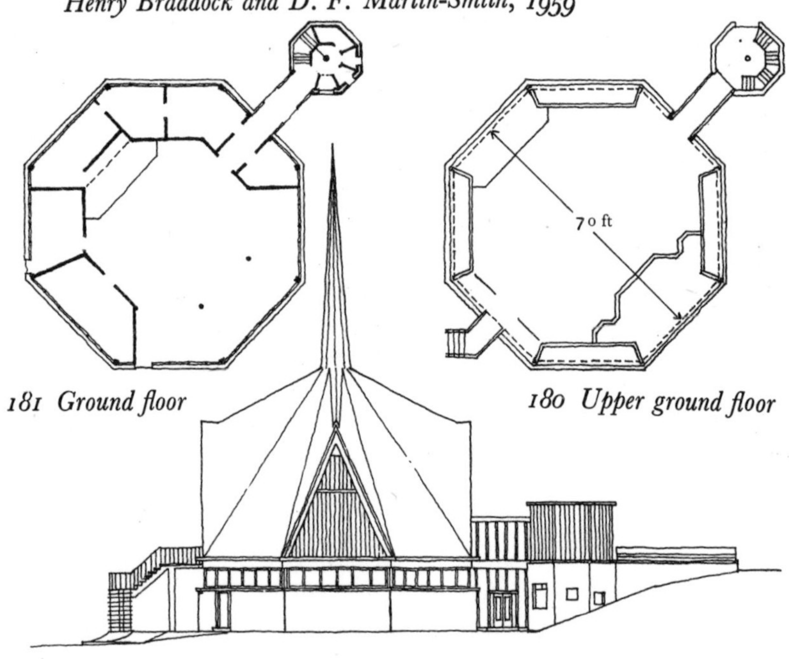

181 Ground floor

180 Upper ground floor

179 North east elevation St Andrew's Sidcup, Kent
Henry Braddock and D. F. Martin-Smith, 1965

Glossary

Abacus:	the flat slab on the top of a capital
Apse:	a vaulted or semi-circular end of a chancel or chapel
Battlement:	a parapet with a series of regular indentations crenellated as on a castle wall
Boss:	a carved keystone at the junction of two or more ribs of a vault
Capital:	a head or top part of a column
Clerestory:	the side wall above the aisle roof and nave arcade, usually pierced with windows
Corbel:	a projecting stone bonded into a wall to carry a weight
Crocket:	a decorative feature carved in various leaf forms at regular intervals on the sloping sides of spires, pinnacles and gables
Crossing:	the space at the intersection of chancel, transepts and nave
Cupola:	a small domed turret crowning a roof
Diaper work:	surface decoration composed of square or lozenge shapes
Dripstone or Hood-mould:	a projecting moulding placed for protection around the arch of a window or doorway
Finial:	a carved foliage crowning a pinnacle or gable
Foliated:	carved with leaf shapes
Impost:	brackets in walls usually formed of mouldings on which the ends of an arch rest
Jamb:	the straight side of an archway, doorway or window
Keystone:	the middle stone in an arch, often prominent and decorated

Moulding: the contour given to a projecting part of a construction to produce a contrast of light and shade

Mullion: a vertical stone strut dividing windows into two or more lights

Ogee: the shape produced by a concave and convex curve flowing one into the other

Parapet: low wall of a building arising above the level and eaves of a roof

Parclose: a screen enclosing a chapel

Pier: a mass of masonry built up in courses and supporting one or more arches

Pilaster: a flat strip or column attached to a wall

Pinnacle: an ornamental form crowning a spire, tower or buttress, usually conical or pyramidal in shape

Piscina: a water drain in the wall near the altar

Plinth: a projecting base of a column or wall

Quoins: shaped stones at the corners of buildings

Reredos: a structure behind the altar, usually of carved wood or alabaster

Rustication: the placement of large blocks of stone, rectangular or V-shaped, at door and window surrounds to give impression of added strength

Sedilia: seats for priests carved into south wall of chancel

Shaft: a small thin column

String course: a projecting band or moulding carried round a building marking its stages

Tracery: ornamental stonework in heads of Gothic windows

Transom: a horizontal bar across a window

Tympanum: the filling of the arch of a Norman doorway

Wall Construction

82 *Long and short work*

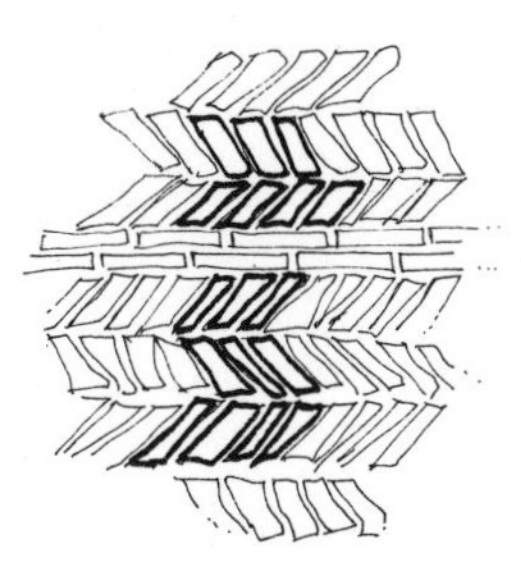

183 Herringboning

184 Crude wall construction with core of rubble

Vaulting

185 Barrel vault

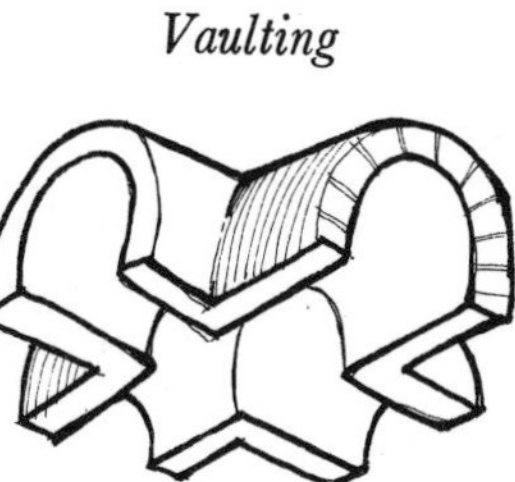

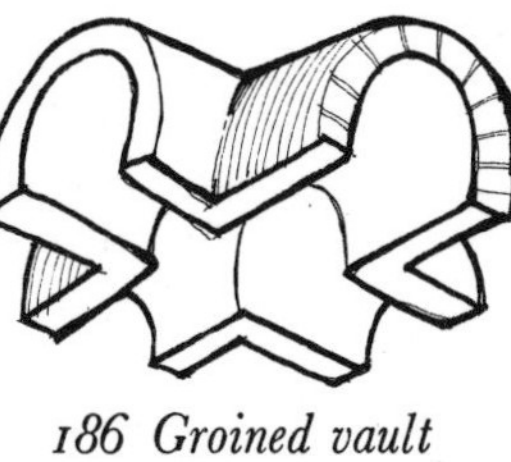

186 Groined vault

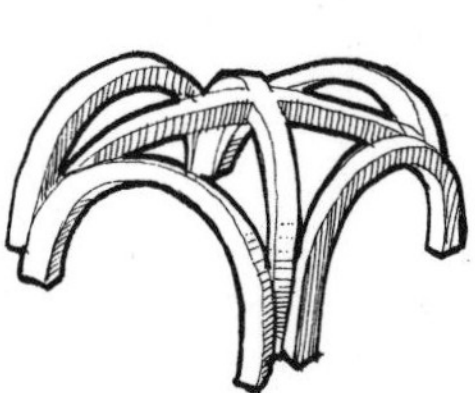

187 Ribbed vault

188 Ribbed vault with pointed arch

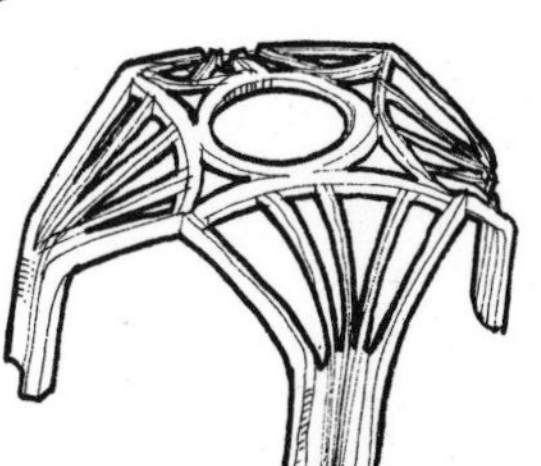

189 Fan vault

Roof Construction

190 Tie beam with king post truss

191 Wagon roof

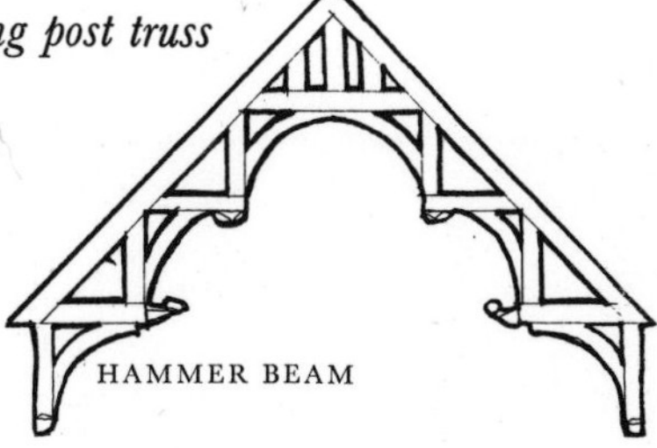

192 Double hammer beam

Bibliography

Betjeman, John *Collins Guide to English Parish Churches* William Collins and Sons Ltd

Bloxham, Matthew H. *Principles of Gothic Ecclesiastical Architecture* Volume I George Bell and Sons

Bond, Francis *Gothic Architecture in England* B. T. Batsford Ltd

Clarke, Basil and Betjeman, John *English Churches* Vista Books

Cook, G. H. *The English Mediaeval Parish Church* Phoenix House Ltd

Cox, J. Charles and Ford, Charles Bradley *The Parish Churches of England* B. T. Batsford Ltd

Dutton, Ralph *The Age of Wren* B. T. Batsford Ltd

Fletcher, Sir Bannister *A History of Architecture on the Comparative Method* Sixteenth edition B. T. Batsford Ltd

Godfrey, Walter H. *The Story of Architecture in England* Volumes I and II B. T. Batsford Ltd

Hammond, Peter (Editor) *Towards a Church Architecture* The Architectural Press

Incorporated Church Building Society *Sixty Post-War Churches* Incorporated Church Building Society

Kersting, A. F. and Vale, Edmund *A Portrait of English Churches* B. T. Batsford Ltd

Mee, Arthur *The King's England* (Wiltshire) Hodder and Stoughton Ltd

Needham, A. *How to Study an Old Church* B. T. Batsford Ltd

Parker, John Henry *Introduction to Gothic Architecture* James Parker and Co. 1877

Pevsner, Nicholas *The Buildings of England* Penguin Books

Rickman, Thomas *Styles of Architecture in England* Sixth edition John Henry and James Parker 1862

Vale, Edmund and Mansbridge, John *Churches* Junior Heritage Books B. T. Batsford Ltd

Yarwood, Doreen *The Architecture of England* B. T. Batsford Ltd

Index

Index to places

The numerals in **bold** refer to illustrations

Index to architects and designers

The numerals in **bold** refer to illustrations